THE GOLF ROUND
I'LL NEVER FORGET

Second Edition

THE GOLF ROUND
I'LL NEVER FORGET

Golf's Biggest Stars Recall
Their Finest Moments

MATT ADAMS

FIREFLY BOOKS

A FIREFLY BOOK

Published by Firefly Books Ltd. 2024
Copyright © 2024 Firefly Books Ltd.
Text copyright © 2019, 2024 Matt Adams
Photographs © as listed on page 206

First printing

Library of Congress Control Number: 2023947695

Library and Archives Canada Cataloguing in Publication
Title: The golf round I'll never forget : golf's biggest stars recall their finest moments /
    Matt Adams.
Other titles: Golf round I will never forget | I'll never forget
Names: Adams, Matthew E., 1964- author.
Description: Second edition. | Includes index.
Identifiers: Canadiana 20230551459 | ISBN 9780228104612 (softcover)
Subjects: LCSH: Golfers—Anecdotes. | LCSH: Golf—Anecdotes. |
    LCSH: Golfers—Biography. | LCGFT: Anecdotes. | LCGFT: Biographies.
Classification: LCC GV964.A1 A33 2024 | DDC 796.352092/2—dc23

Published in the United States by
Firefly Books (U.S.) Inc.
P.O. Box 1338, Ellicott Station
Buffalo, New York 14205

Published in Canada by
Firefly Books Ltd.
50 Staples Avenue, Unit 1
Richmond Hill, Ontario L4B 0A7

Cover and interior design: Matt Filion
Additional writing: Domenic Scarano

Printed in China | E

CONTENTS

INTRODUCTION

By the time I entered the tiny house near the 18th green at Bay Hill Club and Lodge in Florida, the camera crew had already set up for the interview.

The house itself was cute and cozy. The latch on the front door was rather loud, so everyone in the room turned to look the next time the door began to open. The bright morning sun illuminated the door's edges, and by the time it was fully opened, the sun formed a silhouette around the man who even now was impossible to confuse with any other — Arnold Palmer.

Mr. Palmer shuffled down the short hall with labored steps. I was concerned he might trip on the rug or some of the video equipment. However, in contrast to the frailty of his physical movement, his persona was as strong as ever; no one dared ask if he needed assistance. Mr. Palmer sat down heavily in the high-back chair and exhaled slightly, his effort rewarded with this respite.

"I used to live in this house," he said quietly as he took in his surroundings.

Well into his 80s then, and still among golf's highest-grossing personalities, Mr. Palmer lacked any sense of pretense. He could afford to live anywhere, but instead he quietly said, "I'm thinking of moving back in."

This interview I conducted with Mr. Palmer would end up being his last long-form, sit-down interview. We spoke at length about his 1960 come-from-behind victory at the U.S. Open (which you can read about on page 65). His recollections were priceless, and it was clear this man was more than a legend — he was a bridge to professional golf's earliest days. From Gene Sarazen, Walter Hagen and Bobby Jones through to Ben Hogan, Gary Player, Jack Nicklaus and many other modern champions, Mr. Palmer was a link. "Walter asked me to be a pallbearer at his funeral and I was. Bob Jones told me that if his life depended on one putt, he would want me to make it. Isn't that neat?"

It was. My interview with Mr. Palmer is one of my all-time favorites. I've spent my entire career working in golf on both the equipment and grass sides of the game. Broadcasting, however — which started as a hobby — soon became my primary employment. I've had the pleasure of conducting more than 10,000 interviews as the host of my radio show, *Fairways of Life*. I started the show simply because I knew there were many people who shared a tremendous passion for the game that went beyond the course. Every person contains a personal library full of hopes, heartaches, successes and failures. I've always believed that getting people to open up and share their stories has a larger benefit: somewhere, someone may be dealing with something similar. Finding comfort in knowing others have dealt with similar circumstances can be the most powerful medicine in the world. I wanted to explore that through golf.

Some of the recent stories in this book originated from my show, but more often, the stories contained here were pulled from occasions that were even more personal. I've had the

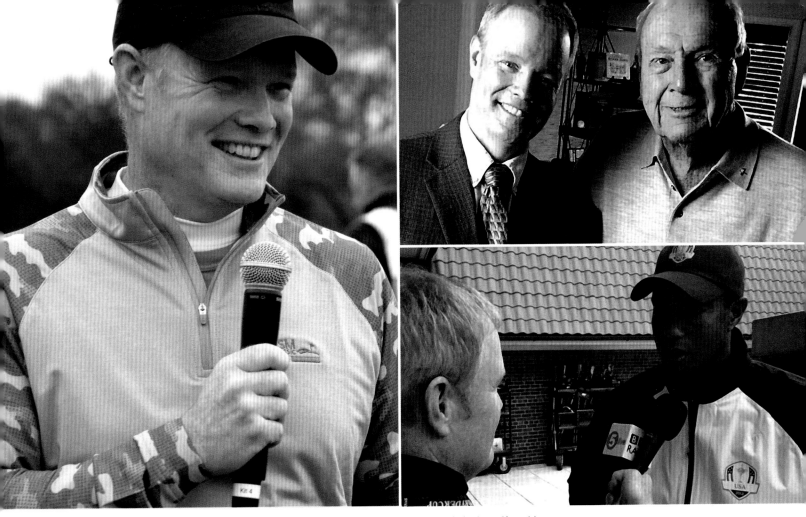

Matt Adams, "golf's best interviewer," has done more than 10,000 interviews with people in the golf world, including legends Arnold Palmer (top right) and Tiger Woods (bottom right).

privilege of being with golf legends over dinners, in airplanes and while playing. The oldest story in this book that came about in this fashion is Gene Sarazen's albatross at the 1935 Masters. I was introduced to him at a restaurant in the mid-1990s when he was in his mid-90s. It was a once-in-a-lifetime opportunity.

So too was having a front-row seat for Jordan Spieth's win at the 2017 Open at Royal Birkdale. I was assigned to do the play-by-play for the world radio feed. Other than Spieth and Matt Kuchar and their caddies, I could not have been closer to the action. So close, in fact, that at one point I thought I might cost Spieth his chance at victory.

After the now famous delay at the

13th hole on Sunday, I desperately needed to use the facilities. My broadcast partner, Paul Eales, assured me there was a "port-a-loo" before the 14th tee. After we all finally cleared from the 13th, I let the army pass by and found my place of relief. The audio of the live broadcast was playing in my headset, so I knew Jordan had struck his tee shot at the par-3 14th. Thinking I had all the time in the world, I suddenly heard a loud series of knocks on the plastic door. Startled, I cracked open the door to be greeted by the face of Jordan Spieth! Obviously, he suffered similarly, and he surely did not want to unduly delay Kuchar and The Open any further.

I hurriedly got out of the way. Moments later Spieth emerged and

galloped down the slope toward the green, while I whispered a silent prayer that the port-a-loo delay would not put him off enough to miss the golden birdie opportunity that awaited him. Thankfully he made it, and his torrid finish, outlined in this book (find it on page 58), became that of lore.

Each of these stories has special meaning. My hope is that in their recounting you will find a connection not only to the story told but also to the human being who was able to rise above the improbability, fear, insecurities and obstacles that stood in the way of their accomplishment, thereby inspiring you to achieve your own life's goals, be they great or small.

— Matt Adams

HISTORY IN THE MAKING

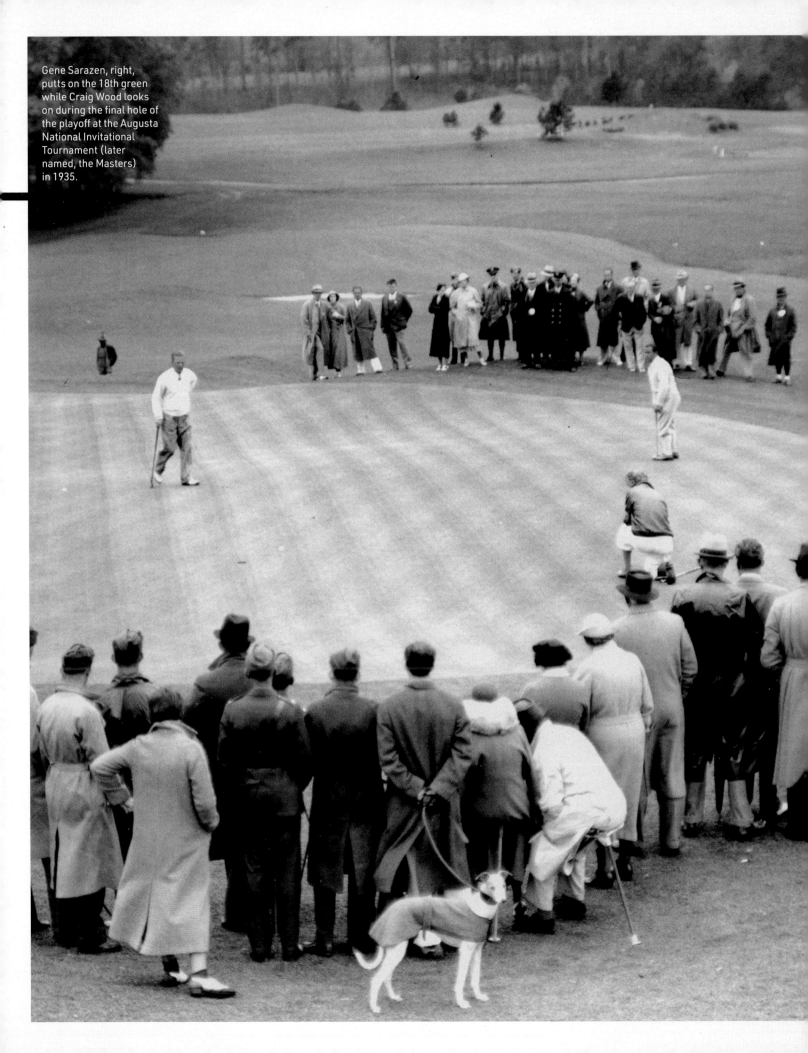

Gene Sarazen, right, putts on the 18th green while Craig Wood looks on during the final hole of the playoff at the Augusta National Invitational Tournament (later named, the Masters) in 1935.

GENE SARAZEN

THE SHOT HEARD 'ROUND THE WORLD

⚑

1935 MASTERS TOURNAMENT

FINAL ROUND

You know you've just made sports history when the press has to invent a word to describe your heroics. Such was Gene Sarazen's incredible shot on the 15th hole at the 1935 Masters, rivaled in drama, timing and impact perhaps only by Tiger Woods' chip-in for birdie on the 16th hole in 2005. Sarazen's shot not only changed golf's lexicon, it put Augusta on the sports map and, in hindsight, made him golf's first winner of the modern Grand Slam.

Gene Sarazen poses for a photo at the Augusta National Invitational Tournament in 1935.

He followed that up with a 71 and then a 73 after rain arrived for the third round. Heading into the final round, Sarazen stood in fourth place at 4 under par, three shots behind the leader, Craig Wood.

In an era before modern pairing considerations (such as television), Wood actually teed off four groups in front of Sarazen, who was paired with Walter Hagen. Wood would post a 3-over 39 going out, which gave hope to the pursuers chasing him. Taking advantage, Sarazen started strong and, at one point, was tied for the lead before bogeys on the 9th and 10th holes dropped him back. Wood, who had finished second in the inaugural event, had steadied himself by picking up two strokes to par on the back side through the 17th hole.

Meanwhile Hagen and Sarazen were starting the 485-yard par-5 15th hole, with Sarazen trailing Wood by two strokes. The fairway before him sloped from right to left, and he launched a long drive that used the hole's contour to his advantage. It settled near the crest of the hill some 235 yards from the green.

As Hagen and Sarazen reached their balls, they heard a roar from the 18th green echoing through the pines.

W hat if your entire career was remembered for one climactic moment?

Such was the case for the legendary Gene Sarazen, author of one of the most famous shots in Masters history: a double eagle on the par-5 15th hole.

The feat took place in 1935 and is said to have put the Masters on the map of the world sports stage. Although this perspective has its merits, it should be viewed in its appropriate historical perspective.

It was just the second year of the Masters, and Sarazen had missed the inaugural tournament because of a commitment to play in a series of exhibitions in South Africa with Joe Kirkwood, an infamous trick-shot artist. Today a golfer would be criticized for passing up an invitation to the Masters to play an exhibition. But in 1934 it was simply known as the Augusta National Invitational Tournament. It wouldn't become known by its more famous moniker for another few years.

Sarazen made sure he was there the following year. He started the 1935 tournament with a solid 68.

1935 MASTERS TOURNAMENT **FINAL ROUND**	ROUND 1	ROUND 2	ROUND 3	ROUND 4	TOTAL
	68	71	73	70	**282**

HOLE	1	2	3	4	5	6	7	8	9	10	11	12	13	14	15	16	17	18	TOTAL
PAR	4	5	4	3	4	3	4	5	4	4	4	3	5	4	5	3	4	4	**72**
SARAZEN	4	4	4	4	4	3	4	5	5	5	4	3	4	4	2	3	4	4	**70**

Wood had birdied the 18th. Sarazen's deficit now stood at three strokes.

Upon hearing the news, Hagen reportedly said, "Well, that's that," and played his second shot safely before the water fronting the green.

Sarazen, meanwhile, surveyed his options. He decided that going for the green was his only choice if he was to shave three strokes over the final four holes and catch Wood. His ball lay behind a small crest in the hill in a slight depression, and he asked his caddie, who went by the nickname "Stovepipe," what club he should hit.

"Stovepipe suggested a full 3-wood, but I determined I needed a 4-wood, given the lie," Sarazen said.

Before hitting the shot, Sarazen rubbed his good-luck ring off Stovepipe's forehead for a little extra luck. The ring had been given to him by a friend who claimed it once belonged to Mexican president Benito Juarez. The president was said to have been wearing the ring the night he was elected (though this account is widely disputed).

Sarazen was renowned as a fast player, and he took little time over the shot. Toeing the club to decrease its loft, he lashed at the ball with a swing that distinguished him as a power golfer, despite his 5-foot-4 frame.

"When I hit it," he said, "I just had a feeling."

Sarazen's ball narrowly cleared the water, bounced onto the putting surface, then rolled right to left directly toward the pin before diving into the hole. Contrary to popular belief, there were only a couple dozen patrons surrounding the green at the time. Among them was Bobby Jones, the sport's reigning icon, who would end up tied for 25th. Sarazen later noted that one of the most satisfying things about making the shot was that both Jones and Hagen were there to witness it.

When word of what happened got back to the clubhouse, it was met with shock. Members of the media had been congratulating Wood, and the $1,500 winner's check had reportedly been drawn out to him already. Sarazen's shot caused an additional conundrum for the media — they didn't know what to call 3 under par on one hole. They convened and eventually decided on "double eagle" over other suggestions, such as "twin dodo."

After his historic shot, Sarazen still had work ahead of him to maintain his share of the lead. He parred the 16th and 17th holes, but at the uphill 18th he struck an uncharacteristically weak drive that resulted in his calling on the services of his heroic 4-wood once again to reach the green. Two putts later he'd lived to play another day.

The next day, Sarazen and Wood went head-to-head over 36 additional holes — the only such playoff in the tournament's history. It appeared fate was already on Sarazen's side, and the results were a testament to it as he soundly defeated Wood by five strokes.

Viewed in retrospect, that victory means Sarazen is the first man to accomplish the modern Grand Slam. Of course, this distinction wasn't noted until many years later. The Augusta National Invitational Tournament wasn't looked upon as a major at that time, and the concept of the Grand Slam didn't take shape until the dominating years of Ben Hogan.

Nonetheless, now known as an albatross, Sarazen's spectacular 3-under-par shot not only defined his career but also helped lay down a major foundation.

Johnny Miller celebrates
a putt during his
record-setting round of
63 at the 1973 U.S. Open.

JOHNNY MILLER
A SHOCKING RECORD

1973 U.S. OPEN

FINAL ROUND

After three rounds at Oakmont, both Arnold Palmer and Jack Nicklaus remained in the hunt. So on Sunday morning the golf world awoke expecting nothing less than another showdown between the two legends. What it got instead was perhaps the greatest final round at a major. Johnny Miller, six shots back of the lead and urged on by a mysterious voice, came from behind to set a course record 63 to win his first U.S. Open in striking fashion.

Johnny Miller throws his ball into the crowd after winning the 1976 Open. Miller's win at The Open was his second victory at a major tournament.

Coming into the 1973 U.S. Open at Oakmont, all eyes were on defending champion Jack Nicklaus and 43-year-old Arnold Palmer. And after three rounds the level of excitement had reached a fevered pitch.

Palmer shared the lead with three others, including 1952 and 1963 U.S. Open champion Julius Boros, who was 53 years old. Tom Weiskopf, who would win The Open one month later, was one stroke behind. Nicklaus was four shots back but still very much in the picture.

Everyone expected Palmer to come out firing at every pin, but everybody also knew Nicklaus wouldn't just roll over. What no one in the golf world expected was that a 26-year-old two-time PGA Tour winner by the name of

Johnny Miller would end up stealing the show from the game's biggest stars.

Yet Miller did have one supporter, of sorts. All week he had been followed by a woman claiming to be a psychic and "knowing" he would win the tournament. And then in his locker before the final round, Miller said he found a letter postmarked from Iowa that simply said, "You are going to win the U.S. Open." No name, no return address.

Ahead of the fourth round, however, not even Miller himself held out any hope. He woke up Sunday morning six shots behind the leaders and separated by 12 hungry players. So Miller told his wife to be packed and ready to go immediately following his final round. He figured after his 76 the day before — when the rest of the leaders were

moving in the other direction — he was merely managing his expectations.

"I was just kind of going through the motions on the practice tee," Miller said. "Everybody and their dog was ahead of me on the leaderboard, and they were all the stars of the day . . . I'm like, 'I've got no chance.'"

On the practice tee, however, the strange happenings that week continued for Miller. He claimed that an unrelenting "voice" within him was urging him to open his stance. It was a compulsion he couldn't ignore.

"The voice was very clear, so much so I was a bit startled," Miller said. "I wondered if I should actually open my stance that much on the course, but as far back as I was I didn't think I had anything to lose."

Miller teed off one hour ahead of the leaders and got off to a great start with four straight birdies. Just like that he was 4 under on the day. All of a sudden the prospect of winning didn't seem so foreign to him.

"So far the little voice in my head was right," Miller said. "I'm right in this. But this reality made me a little tight, and I started leaving putts short."

Pars on the next three holes brought him back to reality. Then he bogeyed the 8th to drop to –3 for the day and even par for the tournament.

1973 U.S. OPEN FINAL ROUND										ROUND 1	ROUND 2		ROUND 3		ROUND 4		TOTAL	
										71	69		76		63		**279**	
HOLE	1	2	3	4	5	6	7	8	9	10	11	12	13	14	15	16	17	18	TOTAL
PAR	4	4	4	5	4	3	4	3	5	4	4	5	3	4	4	3	4	4	**71**
MILLER	3	3	3	4	4	3	4	4	4	4	3	4	2	4	3	3	4	4	**63**

"I got mad after that and it woke me up, made me settle down," Miller said. "From then on I felt a sense of confidence, like I could put the ball wherever I wanted to. From there I hit every green and missed only one drive. I couldn't wait to hit the next shot."

Miller made birdie on the 9th hole and then parred the 10th. At the 11th hole he wedged his approach to 15 feet and made another birdie to move within striking distance of the lead.

"Coming into the round, my play was just okay," Miller said. "This round was really out of nowhere."

About this time the leaders were finishing up their front nine in what was a frenzied final round. Palmer and Boros continued to fight the good fight, and through nine they held a share of the lead with Weiskopf.

Some measure of adversity struck Miller on the 603-yard par-5 12th hole. His drive found the rough, and the most club he could get on the ball was a 7-iron from the lie. He now needed to hit a 4-iron to reach the green. But Miller stuck it to within 15 feet of the flag and converted the putt. He now stood at 6 under for the day and 3 under for the tournament.

Word of Miller's historic pace began to filter through the course. In an attempt to catch history in the making, the gallery started to surge across the footbridge that spanned the Pennsylvania Turnpike to catch a glimpse. So determined were the frenzied legions that some even crawled across the foot-wide railing as traffic zoomed beneath them.

Miller's 4-iron was an asset again on the 13th hole when he used it to laser his approach to 5 feet and convert yet another birdie. He was now tied for the lead with Palmer at 4 under. Miller left his birdie putt on the 14th hole an inch from dropping, which set up a dramatic 15th.

The 453-yard par-4 15 was intimidating not only for its length but also for its 34-yard-wide fairway and bunkers on each side. Playing as if fate had found its hero, Miller hit his drive some 275 yards, splitting the bunkers and hitting the fairway. He then struck his trusty 4-iron shot to within 10 feet of the pin. His birdie putt was dead center, and with it he owned sole possession of the lead at 5 under par.

After parring the 16th and 17th holes, Miller unleashed a huge drive

(and a final exclamation point) on the par-4 18th, leaving him only a 5-iron to get home.

"The hole was back-right, but my ball got held up on a tier," Miller said. "My putt for a 62 lipped out, and after a tapping in, I became the first player ever to shoot a 63 in the final round of a major."

Miller finished the day with a 32 on the front nine and a 31 on the back side, having hit every green in regulation. Forced to wait out the players still on the course, Miller knew his fate was no longer in his hands. But none of his pursuers could catch him. John Schlee finished in second place and Weiskopf in third; Palmer and Nicklaus tied with Lee Trevino for fourth. Miller had won his first U.S. Open.

"To shoot a 63 in the final round of the U.S. Open and to do it the way I did was really special," Miller said. "My dad used to tell me I was going to win the U.S. Open some day, and here I had done it. It changed me. The next year I won eight times."

When asked about the mysterious woman's premonition, Miller said simply, "I guess she was right."

AL GEIBERGER

MR. 59

⚑

1977 DANNY THOMAS MEMPHIS CLASSIC

SECOND ROUND

The year 1977 featured four of golf's most enduring majors, including a pair of showdowns between Jack Nicklaus and Tom Watson. Perhaps lost in all the major drama that year, however, was Al Geiberger's 59 at the Danny Thomas Memphis Classic. In the parochial world of golf, his record was as significant as Roger Bannister's breaking the four-minute mile, even if Geiberger didn't immediately get the recognition he deserved. It was a mark that stood for nearly four decades. The oppressive heat and humidity Geiberger had to fight through to set the record makes the mark all the more impressive.

T he 1977 Danny Thomas Memphis Classic had a curious feeling to it from the beginning. President Gerald Ford, noted for his capacity to hit wild shots, made a hole in one in the tournament's Pro-Am, which fired up the crowd. Then when the professional tournament got under way, Mother Nature delivered stifling heat to add to the test for golf's best, with most days climbing to nearly 100°F (38°C) by mid-afternoon.

In the hot, dry and overbearing heat at the Colonial Country Club in Memphis, 39-year-old Al Geiberger posted a 72 in his first round, sitting well back of leader Tom Storey's 65.

"It was so hot and miserable that I was just trying to survive," Geiberger said. "During the second round a fire started in one of the fields where they parked cars. The fire burned up eight cars," he recalled. "I remember the smoke going straight up, so I could use it to tell which direction the wind was going."

Beginning his second round on the 10th hole, Geiberger started with an eagle and two birdies. He then went on a bit of a run, going 5 under par over his next nine holes. After 12 holes of play he was already –9 for the day.

Pars on the next two holes briefly halted his hot streak. But on the next tee Geiberger regrouped and hit a perfect drive.

He hit his approach to about 10 feet and made the birdie putt.

Geiberger birdied the next two holes as well. Then on the final hole, number 9 on the course, he had an 8-foot birdie putt for a spot in golf history.

"The grain was in to me and across at the same time," Geiberger said. "Worst combo, as it's going to affect the putt a great deal. Somehow I got it to drop."

Geiberger had done it. He was the first player to shoot a 59 on the PGA Tour.

There are two things the history books generally skip over about that day. The first is that Geiberger used the same ball the entire round, which was unheard of in those days. "With a wound ball, often I'd switch after only three holes as the ball would crack or get out of round," Geiberger recalled. "But that day I was pretty superstitious!"

The other overlooked fact is that Geiberger's record-setting round didn't ensure a win that week. In the third round he shot another 72, which cut his six-shot lead in half. Then halfway through the final round, Gary Player had actually taken over the lead.

"It was a lot of work to come back and win the tournament," he said. "Everyone told me I had to win the tournament because I shot 59."

Al Geiberger watches a putt at a tournament in the late 1970s.

Despite another hot, humid, miserable day, Geiberger was able to somehow gather himself and regroup. He came back with a 32 on the back side and ended up winning by three strokes.

Surprisingly Geiberger's record didn't immediately get the recognition it so deserved.

"Funny thing is, when I had the 59 not many people talked about it, there wasn't much attention," Geiberger said. "About a month later, other players started calling me 'Mr. 59.' In the next couple of years it became more popular."

In the decades that followed, a handful of players had tied the mark, but no one had beaten it. Then in 2016 some friends were planning a big celebration for the 40th anniversary of Geiberger's record round when Jim Furyk popped out a 58 at the Travelers Championship.

So Geiberger's record has been broken, but he takes solace in the fact that he was the first player with a sub-60 round.

"I'll always be the first to do what I did," Geiberger said. "And it's fun to think about it."

1977 DANNY THOMAS MEMPHIS CLASSIC **SECOND ROUND**										ROUND 1			ROUND 2			ROUND 3		ROUND 4	TOTAL
										72			59			72		70	**273**
HOLE	10	11	12	13	14	15	16	17	18	1	2	3	4	5	6	7	8	9	TOTAL
PAR	5	4	3	4	3	4	5	4	4	4	4	3	4	4	3	5	4	5	72
GEIBERGER	3	3	2	4	3	3	4	4	3	3	4	2	4	4	2	4	3	4	59

LANNY WADKINS

ALL OF A SUDDEN DEATH

1977 PGA CHAMPIONSHIP

PLAYOFF

Collecting more than 20 PGA Tour wins over the course of a career is quite an accomplishment.
So special, in fact, that in the history of the game only 33 men have done it. Lanny Wadkins is one of them.
He amassed 21 victories on the PGA Tour during his career, none more memorable than the
1977 PGA Championship. It was his only major, but Wadkins made it count, winning in
dramatic fashion in a sudden-death playoff at Pebble Beach.

Heading into the PGA Championship in 1977, Lanny Wadkins wasn't even close to being the tournament favorite. Tom Watson had won five times that year, including the Masters and The Open. Jack Nicklaus was still dominating and would win three times. Ben Crenshaw, Raymond Floyd and Lee Trevino were also winning events.

The tournament that year was held in August at the iconic Pebble Beach Golf Links in California. The state was going through an unprecedented drought that summer, and it clearly affected the course.

"It was playing extremely fast," Wadkins said. "I hit clubs at some of those holes I have never hit before or since."

But that wasn't the only challenge the players faced as they reached the final round. The wind, which had behaved itself all tournament, had begun to pick up. That translated into an increase in scoring.

Through the first three rounds, Wadkins found himself tied for fourth with Watson at −4. They were six shots back of the leader, 47-year-old Gene Littler, who had led after every round.

Interestingly enough, the 27-year-old Wadkins didn't actually make a birdie that day until the 18th hole. But he didn't need to. He eagled both par-5s on the front nine, hitting a 2-iron on the 2nd and then a 4-wood on the 6th, both to about 6 feet of the hole.

Littler was solid on the front nine, but whether it was his age, the pressure or just bad luck, things didn't go his way after the turn. He bogeyed five of his first six holes on the back nine, which opened the door for Wadkins.

"All of a sudden, the last three holes I saw the leaderboard and I had a chance."

At Pebble's stunning par-5 18, which hugs the Pacific Ocean on its left all the way in, Wadkins made perhaps his best shot of the round. With a 92-yard approach shot, he dropped the ball 18 inches from the hole for an easy birdie.

"I went, 'Oh my gosh,'" Wadkins said. "I just stepped up to that wedge shot and stuffed it, so that was really cool."

That left Wadkins at −6 as he went into the clubhouse to wait for Littler, who was playing behind him. Littler managed to right himself with pars over the final three holes to tie Wadkins through four rounds.

A major had never been determined by a sudden-death playoff. Unbeknownst to Wadkins, this would be the first.

"At the time we thought it was an 18-hole playoff on Monday, which it had always been," Wadkins said. "I had already had half a beer and they said, 'You are on the tee at 1.' So life changed really quickly."

Lanny Wadkins celebrates a putt in the late 1970s.

The playoff started on the par-4 1st hole and moved to the par-5 2nd. If needed, it would go to the par-4 3rd hole.

Wadkins made a miraculous 12-foot par putt on the 1st hole to stay alive, and both Littler and Wadkins easily birdied the 2nd. So onto the 3rd hole they went.

"It was total chaos for three holes," Wadkins said. "All the gallery ropes were down, people were everywhere . . . it was pretty wild."

After their approach shots landed in the rough, Littler popped out and had a 20-footer for par, while Wadkins chipped out to about 5 feet. Littler missed his putt, leaving Wadkins with a 5-footer for the victory.

With the 1977 PGA Championship hanging in the balance, Wadkins drained the putt. In a moment of unbridled joy, he then leaped two, three, four times as he ran around in celebration.

Over the course of his career, Wadkins finished top-five in 11 major championships, including three second-place finishes at the PGA Championship. His sudden-death win over Littler proved to be his only victory at a major, but for Wadkins it still hasn't lost its luster after all these years.

"The win means so much to me," he said.

1977 PGA CHAMPIONSHIP
PLAYOFF

ROUND 1	ROUND 2	ROUND 3	ROUND 4	TOTAL
69	71	72	70	**282**

HOLE	1	2	3	TO PAR
PAR	4	5	4	
WADKINS	4	4	4	−1
LITTLER	4	4	x	E

CURTIS STRANGE

BACK-TO-BACK CHAMP

⚑

1989 U.S. OPEN

FINAL ROUND

Not since Ben Hogan walked off the South Course at Oakland Hills in Michigan in 1951 had someone captured back-to-back U.S. Open titles. In 1988, Curtis Strange was hot off his best professional year. He won the U.S. Open and finished as the PGA Tour's leading money winner and PGA Player of the Year. When he arrived at Rochester's Oak Hill Country Club for the 1989 U.S. Open, the pressure he felt to perform as a past champion was immense. Known as a tough player who could grind out a win, Strange would need all the resolve he could muster in a tournament that saw him go 35 holes without a birdie.

"**I** was just tickled to death," Curtis Strange said of his being in the hunt on Sunday morning for his second consecutive U.S. Open. "It was great, great pressure — but gosh that's what you practice all those years for."

However, the pressure Strange felt was a little more than just Sunday jitters. Coming in as the defending champion after having won the 1988 tournament in a playoff against Nick Faldo, Strange knew the stakes were somehow higher for him. "The pressure — the demands on yourself — not only physically but mentally . . . there was a lot of weight, a lot of expectation."

Heading into the final round, Strange was sitting at −2, three shots back of the leader, Tom Kite, who was −5.

Strange was a grinder, and he was in the midst of a very long birdie drought. It started on the last two holes of the second round, and it would last through the first 15 holes of the fourth round. Strange had gone 35 holes without a birdie. Fortunately on Sunday, he was keeping himself in the conversation by playing par golf.

"The word was going around that Kite had hit it in the water on 5," Strange recalled. He couldn't believe it. Strange assumed he'd need to go under par on the day to contend, never an easy task at the U.S. Open. But with a shifting

Curtis Strange tees off on the 6th hole at the Oak Hill country club in Rochester, New York, during the final round of the 1989 U.S. Open.

a lot of fortitude and guts . . . It's a marathon in a lot of ways," he reflected.

His drive on 16 found the left side of the fairway, and a wonderfully struck iron shot left him just short and left of the pin. It was a great chance for his first birdie of the day. Standing over the ball in his bright red shirt, he stroked the putt and walked it straight in with a fist pump. "It won the Open for me," Strange said of the birdie putt. "I thought, 'Just put the ball in the fairway and don't panic. Pars will win it for me.'"

With a two-shot cushion now, Strange parred the 17th and bogeyed the 18th for a one-shot victory over Mark McCumber, Chip Beck and Ian Woosman.

Having won the tournament the year prior, Strange knew his mind-set heading into that round was solid, despite the pressure he heaped on himself. "[Winning] helps your self-confidence so much . . . your ability to believe in yourself when that situation comes."

When the situation came, Strange delivered, and when all was said and done, he was a back-to-back U.S. Open champ. Only one player has since equaled the feat — Brooks Koepka in 2017 and 2018.

leaderboard, par was all of a sudden looking pretty good. He was still in the hunt for the championship.

Players will tell you that in a U.S. Open, you need to be ready to take advantage when others falter. It wasn't long before opportunity knocked for Strange. Tom Kite was out of the picture after double-bogeys at the 13th and 15th holes (he would shoot a final-round 78). Strange was still 2 under and had a one-shot lead on Chip Beck as he approached the par-4 16th. A birdie could seal it.

Having strung together pars on the first 15 holes, Strange had had enough. "To go as long as I did without a birdie and to just hang in there, I think it took

1989 U.S. OPEN FINAL ROUND										ROUND 1	ROUND 2	ROUND 3	ROUND 4	TOTAL
										71	64	73	70	**278**
HOLE	1	2	3	4	5	6	7	8	9	10 11 12 13 14 15 16 17 18				TOTAL
PAR	4	4	3	5	4	3	4	4	4	4 3 4 5 4 3 4 4 4				70
STRANGE	4	4	3	5	4	3	4	4	4	4 3 4 5 4 3 3 4 5				70

Tiger Woods holds up the winner's trophy after capturing the 100th U.S. Open Golf Championship on June 18, 2000.

TIGER WOODS

THE TIGER SLAM

2000 TO 2001

FOUR STRAIGHT MAJORS

To win all four majors is a feat of, well, major proportions. To win all four in succession is nearly impossible. But from 2000 to 2001 Tiger Woods did just that, and he did it in unforgettable fashion: Woods won the U.S. Open by 15 strokes at one of America's most important courses, Pebble Beach; at The Open at St Andrews — perhaps the most famous course in the world — he won by eight; at the PGA Championship he won a thrilling playoff over Bob May at Valhalla; and then at the Masters he prevailed in a grinding duel with Phil Mickelson and David Duval. His peers could only watch in awe at the greatness unfolding before their eyes.

Tiger Woods drives from the 12th tee on the final day of the 2000 Open at the Old Course at St Andrews, Scotland.

W hat if the round that can never be forgotten is *rounds* that can never be forgotten? What if the accomplishment was a period of dominance and not merely one round? What if it represents something that had never been done before?

Although it wasn't the Grand Slam — winning all four majors in one calendar year — Woods' historic run remains unmatched in golf history. It's still the only time a player has won all four majors in succession. Sportswriters dubbed it the Tiger Slam.

Woods himself was bowled over by what he had accomplished.

"The first two that I won probably could not have happened on two better sites," he said. "It's not too often you get to play Pebble Beach and St Andrews. Pebble Beach is probably the greatest golf course we have over here, and St Andrews is probably the greatest course in the world.

"And to win at Valhalla under those conditions, having to make birdie after birdie after birdie, just to hang in there, that was tough. And then to do it [at Augusta National] . . . again, one

of the most historic sites in all of the world, it's pretty neat."

The story begins in 2000 at Pebble Beach with the 100th U.S. Open. Woods had competed for the national title five times to that point, his best finish a tie for third in 1999. In 2000 he opened with a 65, just one shot better than Angel Cabrera. Then in the second round, Woods posted a 69 on a day when the average score was almost 76. He would've done even better, but on the 18th hole he deposited his drive in the Pacific Ocean and went on to make double-bogey. Even with that mishap, his lead was still six strokes.

The third round was a huge eye-opener. The field hit only 43 percent of the greens as the winds off the Pacific soared. Woods had an adventure at the 3rd hole, where he made triple-bogey, but that was the exception. He hit 12 of a possible 14 fairways to battle his way to a 1-over 71. Ernie Els was the only golfer to shoot better on the day, and still Woods led the tournament by a whopping 10 shots.

"I knew that if I shot even par or something close to that, I'd pick up a shot or two just because the conditions were so severe out there," Woods said when he came off the course Saturday. Little did he know at the time that he had made the fourth round a mere

2000 U.S. OPEN FINAL ROUND										ROUND 1	ROUND 2		ROUND 3		ROUND 4		TOTAL	
										65	69		71		67		**272**	
HOLE	1	2	3	4	5	6	7	8	9	10	11	12	13	14	15	16	17	18	TOTAL
PAR	4	4	4	4	3	5	3	4	4	4	4	3	4	5	4	4	3	5	**71**
WOODS	4	4	4	4	3	5	3	4	4	3	4	2	3	4	4	4	3	5	**67**

2000 OPEN FINAL ROUND										ROUND 1	ROUND 2		ROUND 3		ROUND 4		TOTAL	
										67	66		67		69		**269**	
HOLE	1	2	3	4	5	6	7	8	9	10	11	12	13	14	15	16	17	18	TOTAL
PAR	4	4	4	4	5	4	4	3	4	4	3	4	4	4	5	4	4	4	**72**
WOODS	4	4	4	3	5	4	4	3	4	3	3	3	4	4	4	4	5	4	**69**

formality. On Sunday, his birdies on four of the final nine holes were a coronation of his 15-shot victory.

"He's in another dimension," Els said. "I don't know what we're going to do with him."

Next up was The Open and storied old St Andrews. David Duval posted a mild threat to Woods in the final round, at one point coming within three strokes of the lead with 11 holes to play. But Duval posted a 43 on the final nine after taking four shots in the Road Hole bunker at 17 (Woods, on the other hand, was not once during the tournament in any of St Andrews' 128 bunkers).

Woods breezed home to capture his first Claret Jug. His 269 was the best 72-hole score ever shot at The Open on the Old Course, and he won by eight strokes, the most in any Open since 1913. By virtue of his win at Pebble Beach and St Andrews, Woods had completed his mission of winning all four majors, though not in succession. Amazingly he had done it when he was just 24 years old, in only his fourth year as a professional.

Tom Watson, himself a five-time Open champion, could only admire what he was beholding.

"He's raised the bar to a level only he can reach."

Then it was on to the 2000 PGA Championship held at Valhalla. This one might have been the most satisfying of all Woods' major victories in the Slam. It came in a three-hole playoff battle against one of his heroes, Bob May, a golfing legend in Woods' home turf of Southern California.

Back in a familiar position, Woods was leading going into the fourth round. But by the 4th hole, May had surged into the lead. From that point on the two players staged a brilliant duel to the finish. The turning point came on the 15th hole, with May clinging to a one-shot lead.

Woods had trouble getting to the green, needing three strokes. Once there, he left himself a 12-footer for par, while May needed only a little more than 4 feet for birdie. But Woods coaxed in his putt while May missed. May's lead was still just one stroke.

On the 17th hole, a 422-yarder, Woods blasted his drive to lob-wedge range and made birdie to knot the score. On the 18th, however, May appeared to be in the driver's seat when he made an 18-footer for birdie.

2000 PGA CHAMPIONSHIP
FINAL ROUND

	ROUND 1	ROUND 2	ROUND 3	ROUND 4	TOTAL
	66	67	70	67	**270**

HOLE	1	2	3	4	5	6	7	8	9	10	11	12	13	14	15	16	17	18	TOTAL
PAR	4	5	3	4	4	4	5	3	4	5	3	4	4	3	4	4	4	5	**72**
WOODS	4	6	3	4	4	5	4	2	4	4	3	3	4	2	4	4	3	4	**67**

PLAYOFF

HOLE	16	17	18	TO PAR
PAR	4	4	5	
WOODS	3	4	5	–1
MAY	4	4	5	E

2001 MASTERS TOURNAMENT
FINAL ROUND

	ROUND 1	ROUND 2	ROUND 3	ROUND 4	TOTAL
	70	66	68	68	**272**

HOLE	1	2	3	4	5	6	7	8	9	10	11	12	13	14	15	16	17	18	TOTAL
PAR	4	5	4	3	4	3	4	5	4	4	4	3	5	4	5	3	4	4	**72**
WOODS	5	4	4	3	4	3	3	4	4	4	3	4	4	4	5	3	4	3	**68**

Yet Woods again rose to the occasion, curling a 6-foot birdie into the left side of the cup.

"The putt looked scary at first," Woods said. "But then I remember thinking, 'My mother could make this.' And with that thought in my mind I got over the putt and just poured it in."

That sent the pair into a three-hole playoff, mandated for the first time ever by the PGA. Woods birdied the 1st hole with a 20-foot putt while May could only par. Both men made par the 2nd hole. May needed to pick up a stroke to stay alive. His 40-footer for birdie barely missed. Woods, meanwhile, had blasted from a bunker to 2 feet to save par. Suddenly Woods had his third consecutive major. Somewhat lost in the shuffle was the fact that Woods became the first player to defend a PGA Championship since Denny Shute in 1937.

That set the scene for the fourth jewel in the Tiger Slam: the 2001 Masters.

Woods again led heading into the final round, this time by just one shot, with both Phil Mickelson and Duval in hot pursuit. Duval shot a sizzling 32 on the front nine and then added a birdie on the 10th hole to take the

Left: Tiger Woods reacts to making birdie to force a playoff at the 2000 PGA Championship. This page: Woods receives his Masters jacket from Vijay Singh after winning the 2001 tournament.

lead, which he still held as he walked up to the 16th tee.

Woods, playing two groups behind with Mickelson, birdied the 13th, while Duval flew the green with his tee shot on 16. Duval ended with a bogey and Woods took the lead. He would never relinquish it, hanging on tenaciously and dropping in a 16-foot birdie putt on the final hole to win by two strokes.

Woods thus had accomplished something no one else had ever done. Bobby Jones won four "majors" in 1930 in the days before the modern Grand Slam, but his four were the U.S. and British Opens and the U.S. and British Amateurs. Only Woods has been able to win all four of the professional majors in succession.

"It's hard to believe, really, because there are so many things that go into

winning a major championship," Woods said. "For that matter, any tournament, but more so majors, because you've got to have your game peak at the right time. And on top of that, you've got to have some luck. You've just got to have everything kind of go right.

"And to have it happen four straight times, that's awfully nice. Some of the golfing gods were looking down on me the right way."

Morgan Pressel hits a
shot on the 4th hole
during the final round
of the 2007 LPGA
Kraft Nabisco Cup.

MORGAN PRESSEL

MAJOR YOUTH

2007 KRAFT NABISCO CUP

FINAL ROUND

In retrospect, Morgan Pressel's historic win should not have surprised anyone. She had qualified for the U.S. Open in 2001 while she was still 12 and had tied for second at the tournament in 2005 as a 17-year-old. She had received six LPGA sponsor exemptions and never finished lower than 25th in any of them. So when her date with destiny finally arrived in 2007, Pressel was ready for it. Fate made her wait 45 more agonizing minutes to make history, but when it came Pressel shared it with those closest to her. It was a victory she knew would've made her late mother so very proud.

Morgan Pressel, her caddie and her grandmother take the winner's leap into the pond at the 18th hole following her victory at the 2007 Kraft Nabisco Cup.

I n the minds of most people, it wasn't supposed to happen this way. It was supposed to be Michelle Wie striding up the 18th fairway, the victorious teenager in a women's major. If not Wie, perhaps the charismatic Paula Creamer or any one of a dozen other super-talented young golfers from around the world. But it wasn't any of them. It was Morgan Pressel.

Pressel was only 18 years, 10 months and 9 days old when she won the 2007 Kraft Nabisco Cup. It was her first major and her first professional victory, and it earned her a place in golf history as the youngest person ever to win a women's major at the time.

But it sure didn't come easy. To win it Pressel had to play with the nerves of a veteran come Sunday.

"I knew the final round would take everything I had," she said. "I knew I had to play really solid golf and couldn't make mistakes. I had to stay cool and be ready for whatever came at me."

For every dramatic victory, however, there's usually an equally dramatic loss. This time the loser was Norway's Suzann Pettersen, who led by four strokes with just four holes to play. When Pressel completed the final hole after draining a huge 10-foot birdie putt, she was 45 minutes ahead of Pettersen's grouping — an eternity in golf. During that time the world literally changed for both women.

Detractors point out that Pressel wasn't in one of the later groups, so she didn't have to face the demands of being forced to win under the harsh glare of the spotlight. Supporters counter that it was a hot, dry desert day in the Palm Springs area on a golf course that was very difficult. They also point out that it was played at a tournament where the scores are tallied after all 72 holes are played, and that Morgan's age was a disadvantage.

Of course, there is the matter of

2007 KRAFT NABISCO CUP **FINAL ROUND**										ROUND 1	ROUND 2		ROUND 3		ROUND 4		TOTAL		
										74	72		70		69		**285**		
HOLE	1	2	3	4	5	6	7	8	9	10	11	12	13	14	15	16	17	18	**TOTAL**
PAR	4	5	4	4	3	4	4	3	5	4	5	4	4	3	4	4	3	5	**72**
PRESSEL	4	4	4	4	3	4	4	3	5	4	5	3	4	3	4	4	3	4	**69**

Pressel's five key putts on the final nine Sunday. One was a 40-foot bomb for birdie on the 12th hole that really got her round rolling. Three were in the 5-foot range, and the finale was a 10-foot twister on the last hole.

Three of those five putts, on holes 15, 16 and 17, saved par. The slider on 18 was also huge because it gave her a closing birdie and a final score of –3.

"Those were clutch putts I made," she said. "I knew that those were three really big, important putts, probably more important than the putt on 18."

But the final hole was immensely important, no question about it. Pressel pulled a sand wedge from her bag for her approach across the lake to a pin 108 yards away. She placed the shot within the shadow of the flag, just 10 feet away. Her putt died in the heart of the cup, and she was in the clubhouse at 3 under par.

"When I made that putt, I thought, 'That's huge,'" Pressel said. "I knew I really needed that putt."

She still needed a little help, however. After saving par on the 14th hole, Pettersen was four shots ahead of Pressel and three ahead of Se Ri Pak and Catriona Matthew. But all would wilt under Mission Hills' difficult conditions down the stretch.

Pettersen's meltdown began on the 15th hole when she drove into the right rough and made bogey (at the same time Pressel knocked down her birdie at 18). That was compounded by a double-bogey on the 16th after she again lost her drive, then clipped a branch on her escape shot and spun her approach off the green.

While all this was transpiring, Pressel had moved on to the scorer's tent, where there was a TV. She was three shots behind as she finished play, two back when Pettersen began 16. But by the time Pettersen finished the hole, the two were tied. Pressel knew she had a shot at winning, but she could hardly watch.

"You can't control what's going on," she said. "When you're out there and when you're playing, it's a lot easier to control what you do than to wait and see what somebody else does."

On the par-3 17th, Pettersen fell a shot behind when she missed the green with her tee shot and couldn't convert an 8-foot putt for par. She bogeyed the hole to give Pressel the lead.

Pettersen needed to birdie the makeable par-5 18th to force a playoff.

With Pressel barely able to watch, Pettersen missed the fairway with her drive, laid up short of the pond and wedged up to the green. She'd left herself a 25-footer for the tying shot. She lined it up and missed by inches.

"All I remember saying was 'Oh, my God! Oh, my God!'" Pressel said.

After the tumultuous victory, Pressel returned to the 18th green, where she took the traditional winner's leap into the adjacent pond. Despite the singular nature of competing in a golf tournament, major victories are always a culmination of a whole community of supporters. As such Pressel shared the victory with those closest to her. Joining her were her caddie, Jon Yarbrough; her grandmother, Evelyn Krickstein; and her grandfather, Herb Krickstein, who dipped his toes in the water.

Most of all, though, she remembered her mother, Kathy. When Pressel was 15, her mom succumbed to the breast cancer she had been battling for a number of years. She was 43. Pressel couldn't help but break into tears remembering her mother.

"I know my mother is always with me," she said. "And I'm sure she's proud of me."

JIM FURYK
A GROUNDBREAKING 58

2016 TRAVELERS CHAMPIONSHIP

FINAL ROUND

As one of golf's most successful players, Jim Furyk has left a lasting legacy in the sport. He has 26 professional victories, 17 of them on the PGA Tour, including his only major, the 2003 U.S. Open. He's also made a little history along the way, too, thanks to his highly unusual swing. Few can forget his record 12-under 58 in the final round of the 2016 Travelers Championship, where his famously awkward swing was on full display.

J im Furyk's recipe for success has been tenacity mixed with belief and a dash of constant striving to improve. That and his unique swing, which his father honed and which TV analyst and former pro David Feherty once said looked like "an octopus falling out of a tree."

Furyk's proven success with his homegrown swing was underscored in 2013 at the BMW Championship. There he posted a 12-under 59 in the second round, becoming only the sixth golfer to achieve the rare feat on the PGA Tour. Three years later Furyk's habit of making history reached its crescendo when he shot a 12-under 58 in the final round of the 2016 Travelers Championship.

"I felt like someone else leaped into my body and was making the swings," Furyk said of his remarkable performance. And what made it all the more unlikely was that he was struggling to hit consistently. "I hit driver 12 times the day before and hit the fairway, I think, five times?"

But Furyk took his weakness and made it a strength come Sunday. And part of that was a conversation he had the night before with the only coach he's ever had.

"My dad mostly gave me confidence that what I was doing was right," Furyk said. "And he helped with some thoughts on the length of my backswing, which had gotten a little long."

Jim Furyk celebrates after shooting a PGA-record 58 during the final round of the Travelers Championship on Sunday, August 7, 2016.

The pep talk worked. Furyk wound up hitting 13 of 14 fairways on Sunday, and he hit all 18 greens in regulation. He birdied the 2nd hole from 16 feet. On the 3rd hole he was 135 yards from the flagstick, but it was a bit hard to see because of morning shadows from the course's large trees. When he heard his approach shot smack the pin and the handful of people around it cheer, he turned to his caddie, Mike "Fluff" Cowan.

"I said to Fluff, 'I think we made that,'" Furyk recalled.

With the eagle, Furyk was –3 after only two holes. That ignited a torrid stretch as he finished the front nine with an 8-under 27 after his six birdies and an eagle. He took only 10 putts.

"I had the pedal down on the front nine, but I did start running the numbers," Furyk said. "After a while it becomes a mental battle to keep it up . . . I just wanted to stay out of my own way and keep doing what I was doing."

The formula worked as Furyk started the back nine with three straight birdies. That's when adversity set in.

He made a perfect drive on the par-3 13th hole but hit the ball into a divot, forcing him to lay up. Furyk settled for par. He missed a shot at a

birdie on 14 and then another after spinning the ball out of the hole on the drivable par-4 15.

"During that stretch I felt like I was out there for an hour without a birdie," Furyk said.

But Furyk got to the magic number on perhaps the most unlikely hole at TPC River Highlands: the par-3 16th. It plays completely over water to a highly undulating green, and Furyk left himself with a 23-foot putt. Keeping the good times rolling, he curled it into the cup to secure another birdie and reach 12 under par for the round.

"That putt was huge," Furyk said.

"Watching that go in — I was fighting emotions."

A routine par on the 17th hole was ensured after two putts, and he narrowly missed a 57 when his birdie effort on 18 just grazed the cup. But the historic effort was in hand. Furyk had become the first man to post a 58 in an official PGA Tour event. He additionally holds the distinction of becoming the first to shoot multiple sub-60 rounds on the PGA Tour.

"It just goes to show you that no matter how bad you feel you are swinging," Furyk said, "you are never that far away."

2016 TRAVELERS CHAMPIONSHIP
FINAL ROUND

																			ROUND 1	ROUND 2	ROUND 3	ROUND 4	TOTAL
																			73	66	72	58	**269**
HOLE	1	2	3	4	5	6	7	8	9	10	11	12	13	14	15	16	17	18					TOTAL
PAR	4	4	4	4	3	5	4	3	4	4	3	4	5	4	4	3	4	4					**70**
FURYK	4	3	2	3	3	4	3	2	3	3	2	3	5	4	4	2	4	4					**58**

BROOKS KOEPKA

GRINDING IT OUT

⚑

2018 U.S. OPEN

FINAL ROUND

Brooks Koepka won his first U.S. Open by four strokes, tying the record for lowest score ever at the tournament with his –16. His second national championship wouldn't come so easy. The favorable course conditions he enjoyed in 2017 turned downright ugly in 2018, and a nagging wrist injury flared up just before the start of the tournament. For his part, Koepka made no excuses. He wanted to prove his win the year before was no fluke. When it was all over, Koepka would stand shoulder-to-shoulder with two of the game's greatest.

I n brutally tough conditions, Brooks Koepka opened the 2018 U.S. Open with a 75, six shots off the pace. Only four players broke par.

"It was very tough, with winds blowing 20 miles per hour and a lot of crosswinds," Koepka said. "The ball was running out so far on the greens, and some of the putts there was no grass around the hole, so it's hard to stop it."

If the setup at Erin Mills for the 2017 U.S. Open had played right into Brooks Koepka's powerful hands, he wouldn't be so lucky in 2018 at Shinnecock Hills. To become the tournament's first defending champion in 30 years, Koepka would have to do it in vastly different conditions.

"Everyone said that Erin Hills was set up for me," Koepka said. "[Shinnecock Hills, however,] was just back to a typical U.S. Open, where 1 over par wins the golf tournament. It's just a lot of grinding."

Grinding, indeed. Compounding matters for Koepka were the almost four months he spent in an air cast at the start of the year because of a partial tendon tear in his left wrist. Then in May he reinjured the same wrist after he was forced to halt a shot during his downswing when a careless driver zoomed a cart in front of him. Among the crazy rumors that swirled was that a horse chiropractor in Northern Ireland popped the wrist back into place when it acted up.

Brooks Koepka kisses the championship trophy after winning the 2018 U.S. Open, his second consecutive U.S. Open win.

But it seemed like nothing fazed Koepka at the national championship. He posted a second-round 66 to claw back into a five-way tie for fourth place, five shots back of the lead. The third round had plenty of drama. In tough conditions that caused a frustrated Phil Mickelson to hit a putt while his ball was still moving, the United States Golf Association later admitted the course had "gotten away" from them and took the extraordinary step to apologize. Koepka posted a 72, the lowest round among the leaders.

Clearly the USGA intended the course to be receptive to scoring in the final round. Tommy Fleetwood took full advantage, posting a 63 to tie the record for the lowest round ever at the U.S. Open. Koepka charged from the gates, too, with birdies on three of his first five holes to take the lead. He dropped a shot at the next hole but got it back at the 10th.

Yet it was a bogey at the par-3 11th that may have been Koepka's best hole. His pitching wedge off the tee sent his ball bouncing over the small green into the fescue. With the green running away from Koepka, he decided the best play was into a front bunker — which he did. His plan from there was to keep his bunker shot below the hole to leave himself with an uphill putt. Koepka had watched other players hit that putt in the morning and saw a few leave it short, so he knew how slow the green was playing.

"I just told myself to give it a little extra," Koepka said. "The putt I made for bogey was pretty big."

Big putts are particularly big in majors. Koepka parred the next four holes, and grinding out putts was critical. A birdie on the 16th hole gave Koepka a two-shot cushion, and his lead held through his par on the 17th. A bogey at the final hole was enough to secure the win at 1 over par, one stroke better than Fleetwood.

Koepka had secured his place in history, becoming only the third man since World War II to win two straight U.S. Opens, after Ben Hogan (1950 and '51) and Curtis Strange (1988 and '89).

"It's incredible," Koepka said. "To have my name on there twice is pretty incredible, and to go back to back is even more extraordinary. It feels so special. I'm truly honored."

2018 U.S. OPEN **FINAL ROUND**										ROUND 1		ROUND 2		ROUND 3			ROUND 4		TOTAL
										75		66		72			68		**281**
HOLE	1	2	3	4	5	6	7	8	9	10	11	12	13	14	15	16	17	18	TOTAL
PAR	4	3	4	4	5	4	3	4	4	4	3	4	4	4	4	5	3	4	**70**
KOEPKA	4	2	3	4	4	5	3	4	4	3	4	4	4	4	4	4	3	5	**68**

Tiger Woods reacts to his birdie putt on the 15th hole during the second round for the Masters golf tournament.

TIGER WOODS

THE MASTER

2019 MASTERS TOURNAMENT

FINAL ROUND

In 2019, Tiger Woods faced an uphill battle unlike any other in his storied career. The 2019 Masters would prove to be a defining moment, as he aimed to overcome not only a stacked leaderboard but his own physical limitations. This victory was a triumph against all odds, a testament to his unyielding spirit and would solidify his legendary status.

U.S. Open at Torrey Pines in 2008 on a broken leg is Hogan-like in its lasting influence. Tiger's improbable victory at the 2019 Masters, his 5th win at Augusta and 15th major title — secured when age and injury stood as more formidable obstacles than the likes of Brooks Koepka, Dustin Johnson, Xander Schauffele and the rest of the best players in the world —is an accomplishment that is hard to measure. A legend above legends.

Woods started the final round two shots off the lead. To win he would have to do something he had never done in his previous 14 major championships: win from behind. All while playing through a fused back.

"I had serious doubts. I could barely walk. I couldn't sit. Couldn't lay down. I really couldn't do much of anything. Luckily, I had the procedure on my back, which gave me a chance at having a normal life. But then all of a sudden, I realized I could actually swing a golf club again. I felt if I could somehow piece this together that I still had the hands to do it. The body's not the same as it was a long time ago, but I still have good hands. So that certainly has helped, and I pieced it together, and next thing you know, if you look at it, my first 14 wins in majors were always — I had the lead

"C oming here in '95 for the first time and being able to play as an amateur; winning in '97, and then to come full circle, 22 years later, to be able to do it again, and just the way it all transpired. There were so many different scenarios that could have transpired on that back nine. There were so many guys that had a chance to win. The leaderboard was absolutely packed, and everyone was playing well. You couldn't have had more drama. This stuff is hard."

Tiger Woods knows how special his 2019 Masters victory was.

There is no doubt Tiger is amazing, but determining if this was his most impressive major victory is nearly impossible. Consider that he broke barriers, not to mention numerous records, with his breakthrough victory at the Masters in 1997 at just 21. At the U.S. Open at Pebble Beach in 2000, he decimated the competition, winning by an incredible 15 strokes. While the legends of Tiger are almost too numerous to list, winning the

2019 MASTERS TOURNAMENT
FINAL ROUND

										ROUND 1	ROUND 2	ROUND 3	ROUND 4	TOTAL
										70	68	67	70	**275**

HOLE	1	2	3	4	5	6	7	8	9	10	11	12	13	14	15	16	17	18	TOTAL
PAR	4	5	4	3	4	3	4	5	4	4	4	3	5	4	5	3	4	4	**72**
WOODS	4	5	3	4	5	3	3	4	4	5	4	3	4	4	4	2	4	5	**70**

in every one of them, or tied for the lead. To have the opportunity to come back like this, you know, it is probably one of the biggest wins I've ever had for sure because of it."

The turning point seemed to take place at the famed par 3, 12th hole. Before Woods' eyes, one competitor after another found their hopes sunk in Rae's Creek.

"So I just said, just keep plodding along, and then next thing you know, I see Brooksy make a mistake at 12. Francesco made a mistake at 12. Patrick was making a run up ahead. DJ was making a run. Xander was making a run. There were so many different scenarios that evolved, and I was looking at the leaderboard coming off 13 green and there's six, seven guys with a chance to win the tournament. Just kept telling myself, I have, along with Francesco, we have the most holes to play, so whatever they do, I'll just birdie the same holes, then it's a moot point. As you know, I birdied 13, I birdied 15 with two good shots in there, and almost whooped it at 16. That gave me the cush, and I kept telling myself on 17, that tee shot, I said, I've been in this position before. I

had a two shot lead with DiMarco and went bogey, bogey. Let's go ahead and pipe this ball right down the middle. Hit a little flat squeezer out there and I did, I just smoked it. I made par there. Then 18, I said, hey, it's not over yet. Arnold lost the tournament and lost the hole with a double. So let's keep the hammer down. Brooksy could still make birdie up 18 and I could make bogey, and next thing you know we're in a playoff, so let's get this ball in play. I did, and I saw him tap out for par, and that gave me the cush knowing that I could make bogey. And I had a little bit of mud on my golf ball playing that shot, and I said just make sure I overcut this thing; don't undercut it. Overcut it to the right. And I did. I whoofed it and hit it over to the right and I was able to put that ball on the green and two putt."

Woods had done the improbable — some would swear the impossible. Over more than a decade, his unstoppable legend had collapsed into a rubble of incrimination and injury. Apparently, his covenant with fate that would have seen him ascend to the unassailable all-time pinnacle of the sport had been broken. But suddenly,

all the doubt, heartache, healing and hoping seemed to have been rewarded in one of those moments when golf gives you exactly what you want — perhaps exactly what we all needed. Our hero was reinstated, and, for a moment, all seemed possible again. Tiger Woods winning the 2019 Masters was a gift, and if it does not represent the most impressive thing he has ever done in his catalogue of majestic moments, surely it was a victory to walk side-by-side with Jack Nicklaus' in 1986 as the most significant Masters wins ever.

"You never give up. That's a given. You always fight. Just giving up's never in the equation.

Granted, pushing and being competitive has got me into this position, but it's also what got me out of it. I've always had a pretty good work ethic throughout my career and throughout my life, and I just had to change the work ethic a bit and work on some different things. I focused on that and just kept fighting. That's just part of the deal. We wake up every morning, and there's always challenges in front of us, and we keep fighting and keep getting through."

BIG SHOTS AND DEFINING MOMENTS

TOM WATSON
44

TOM KITE
48

HAL SUTTON
50

BUBBA WATSON
52

DAVIS LOVE III
54

HENRIK STENSON
58

JORDAN SPIETH
62

SHANE LOWRY
66

PHIL MICHELSON
70

Tom Watson is all smiles after his victory over Jack Nicklaus at the 1977 Open.

TOM WATSON

HIS DAY IN THE SUN

⚑

1977 U.S. OPEN

FINAL ROUND

No one ever doubted Tom Watson's natural talents. The question was whether he had the mental fortitude to win at the game's highest level. However, even after winning The Open in 1975, his reputation as a choker continued to dog him. To get the recognition he deserved, Watson would have to take on and beat the most feared player in the game: Jack Nicklaus. He did, defeating him at the 1977 Masters. But once wasn't enough for the golf world, so Watson did it again a few months later en route to capturing his second Open title. With glory came the realization of a major champion who had come of age to be known as one of the game's great closers.

A t the 1977 Open, the stage was set for a renewal of the burgeoning Jack Nicklaus–Tom Watson rivalry. Watson had already bested his rival at the Masters earlier in the year, and the golf world was waiting anxiously for another showdown. What it got has been called the greatest final round in major tournament history.

"I felt good," Watson said. "My confidence and expectations were high."

Everyone anticipated that the pair would pick up right where they left off in April. And sure enough, they did. Through the first two rounds at the Turnberry Ailsa Course in Scotland, Watson and Nicklaus posted identical scores of 68 and 70 to sit one stroke off the lead, held by Roger Maltbie. Also tied for second place were Hubert Green and Lee Trevino.

But the third round belonged to Watson and Nicklaus. Paired together, both played brilliant golf, matching each other birdie for birdie in posting matching 65s to lead by three strokes.

Tom Watson and Jack Nicklaus shake hands after Watson's birdie putt to win the 1977 Open. The final-round competition has since been nicknamed the Duel in the Sun.

The fourth round didn't start as anticipated and gave no indication of the drama that would follow. Nicklaus birdied the 2nd hole, while Watson posted a bogey. Nicklaus then birdied the 4th hole to pull ahead by three shots, an often insurmountable lead in the final round of a major.

Watson secured his first birdie of the round at the 5th hole and then made a crucial putt for par at the 6th.

"[It] was a difficult left-to-right putt, the hardest for a right-handed golfer," Watson said. "I made a really good putt there."

Watson birdied the 7th hole and then tied Nicklaus with a birdie on the 8th with a "lucky putt," as Watson called it, as the speed of the ball would have seen it travel well past the hole had it not dropped.

By now the gallery had exploded into a frenzy and needed to be cleared from the fairway at the 9th. After a lengthy delay, Watson bogeyed the hole to fall one shot behind again. He then had to scramble to save par on both the 10th and 11th.

Known for his well-timed attacks, Nicklaus knocked in a 25-foot birdie on the 12th hole to go back up by two strokes. Watson answered, however, with a birdie of his own on 13 to cut the margin back to one. The two each posted pars on the 14th, and Watson then made a remarkable birdie on 15 to square the "mental" match.

Watson had been putting from off the green, 60 feet from the hole, and his ball slammed into the flagstick and dropped.

"At that point I was thinking I'd always wanted to compete against the best, and here I was doing what I had wished for and doing it pretty well," he said. "That birdie changed the momentum of the round. I've had many putts in my career that I call heartbreakers or field goals. It's just a feel thing, and in retrospect I think the putt I made there directly impacted Jack on the 17th green."

After both men parred the 16th hole, the back-and-forth battle moved to 17.

The 17th hole is a relatively short par 5, just under 490 yards, played from an elevated tee to an elevated green. Both men hit perfect drives that split the fairway. But Nicklaus caught his ball heavy and left his second shot well short of the green. Watson placed his second shot on the green, some 15 feet away. Nicklaus negotiated his chip

1977 OPEN FINAL ROUND										ROUND 1	ROUND 2	ROUND 3	ROUND 4	TOTAL
										68	70	65	65	**268**

HOLE	1	2	3	4	5	6	7	8	9	10	11	12	13	14	15	16	17	18	TOTAL
PAR	4	4	4	3	4	3	5	4	4	4	3	4	4	4	3	4	5	4	**70**
WATSON	4	5	4	3	3	3	4	3	5	4	3	4	3	4	2	4	4	3	**65**

to 4 feet from the hole, but his birdie putt slid torturously past the left side. He had to settle for par when he knew he needed more. Watson took the lead for the first time with a two-putt birdie.

The match then moved to the final tee. Up by one shot, Watson informed his caddie he wouldn't be playing it safe, because he expected Nicklaus to make a birdie. Watson's 1-iron played perfectly down the middle of the fairway, leaving a 7-iron to the green.

Nicklaus, crushing into his drive with his trademark power and a "wild" fade flight path, watched his ball settle into the heather beside the fairway. Upon reaching it, he discovered that the ball had actually rolled under some gorse as well.

"I walked over to Jack's ball to see if he had a shot," Watson said. "He was inches from being unplayable. But I knew he had a swing, and I knew the only person in the world who could play that shot was Jack Nicklaus."

Up first, Watson hit one of the finest irons of his entire career — a perfectly struck 7-iron that saw the ball finish some 3 feet from the cup.

"I hit it dead flush," Watson said.

"It was one of the best shots I ever hit. It's something I will never forget."

Down one stroke, under gorse and heather and facing incredible pressure, Nicklaus somehow found a way. He tore at the ball with his 8-iron, blasting ball, earth, heather and gorse to hit a fabulous shot that finished on the edge of the green some 40 feet from the cup.

"It was a mighty swing," Watson said.

In a sight nearly trademarked at The Open, those in the gallery closed in around the competitors, clearly excited to be witnessing history in their midst.

Perhaps the greatest pressure putter the game has ever known, Nicklaus proceeded to add to his legend for making big putts. His 40-foot try for birdie snaked over knolls, breaks and valleys and, remarkably, into the hole.

"Five feet away from the hole I knew it was dead center. That's Jack," Watson said. "The gallery went wild, and I was thinking, 'That's Jack not conceding.' He was going to fight until the end. It was really special."

The pressure now shifted squarely onto the shoulders of Watson. Three feet probably never looked farther.

If his tenacity at the Masters and through 71 holes of this Open weren't enough, finally he had the chance to assert his status as a member of the club that included the greatest golfers the game has ever known.

"The crowd was so fired up that as I lined up my putt, Jack put his hands into the air," Watson said. "They fell silent."

Watson's putt split the hole, securing his birdie, his triumph and a bold new reputation.

"I hit it right-center of the hole, and the Open Championship was mine."

Watson finished with a final-round 65 to Nicklaus' 66. Watson now owned his second Open title and his third major. And with an aggregate score of 268, he had beaten the previous Open record, set by Arnold Palmer in 1962 at Royal Troon, by eight strokes.

A lasting image from The Open came after it was over, when the gracious Nicklaus put his arm around the 10-years-younger Watson as they walked off the green.

"Jack said to me, 'I gave you my best shot, but it wasn't good enough.'"

And one of the greatest rivalries in the history of the game was in full bloom.

TOM KITE

THE ULTIMATE BREAKTHROUGH

⚑

1992 U.S. OPEN

FINAL ROUND

*1992 was truly a season for PGA Tour veterans. Many all-time golfing greats, like Greg Norman,
Ben Crenshaw and Davis Love III, to name a few, were adding to their trophy rooms. In all, there were only
three first-time winners on the Tour that year. Luckily for Kite, he was a seasoned vet himself. By the time the
U.S. Open arrived in June, he had 16 Tour victories and had played in 71 majors, finishing top-10 18 times.
But he had yet to win a major, and the weather at Pebble Beach was wicked. Kite battled the elements and
a packed leaderboard to finally capture his long-coveted crown.*

The morning of the final round of the 1992 U.S. Open, the weather wasn't looking good at the iconic Pebble Beach Golf Links in California. When Tom Kite woke up and stepped outside, he was abruptly met by the unfavorable conditions. It was raining, and the winds were close to 30 mph, with frequent gusts up to 40. It's the sort of circumstances you can't explain to a weekend golfer.

"It's kind of hard to imagine how difficult a golf course like Pebble Beach can be when you get conditions like that," Kite said.

Yet despite the greens being turned "hard as an asphalt parking lot," Kite knew he had an excellent chance to win if he just took his time and trusted himself. It would be a tough day for him, no doubt, but it'd be even tougher for the rest of the field.

Kite was 3 under par heading into the final day, a number he shared with Mark Brooks and Ian Woosnam. Nick Faldo was lurking just one shot back, and they all trailed Gil Morgan, who was 4 under par. Unsurprisingly it was a rocky start for most of the golfers in the final few groups. Faldo shot 77, Woosnam 79 and Morgan disappeared with an 81.

Kite, however, was able to hang in there. Coming off a 20-footer for birdie on a brutal 6th hole, he had a little bit of confidence working. That's when things got interesting.

Tom Kite celebrates a putt during a tournament in the late 1980s.

The 7th hole at Pebble Beach is a short downhill par 3, measuring 107 yards. In simple conditions it's about as benign as a golf hole can get, but conditions were far from simple. Kite had 35 mph winds coming at him. All he could do was play something low to keep it on the green. He tried to play a little punch 6-iron, but the wind took the ball and blew it left of the green.

That left Kite in a very difficult position. It would prove to be an unforgettable moment. It's a shot he'll never forget.

"I had to pitch over the corner of the bunker, and the green was rock hard," Kite said. "Thank goodness the ball rattled the pin and fell right in."

With that, Kite bowed to the crowd with club in hand. He knew there was a lot of golf left to play — and the wind was still howling.

The conditions were so brutal on that Sunday that the average score was 77.3, and 20 of the 66 players in the field didn't even break 80. Kite knew if he could just keep the wheels on, it might be enough.

"I was still in survival mode," he said, "just trying to get in the house."

Colin Montgomerie finished with a 70 early in the day, before the weather became a huge factor, and posted even par for the tournament. Soon afterward Jeff Sluman shot a 71 to finish 1 under par and take the clubhouse lead. Kite just needed another birdie coming in on his back nine and the U.S. Open would be his.

He did more than that. He birdied the 12th hole and added another at the 14th with a dazzling wedge shot that led to a tap-in. When he walked off the 18th green, he had held it together — he posted an even-par 72 in near-impossible conditions for a tournament-winning 3-under-par score. Kite was a U.S. Open champion.

It was the round that defined his career. It would be Kite's only major championship and his ultimate breakthrough.

1992 U.S. OPEN FINAL ROUND										ROUND 1	ROUND 2		ROUND 3		ROUND 4				TOTAL
										71	72		70		72				**285**
HOLE	1	2	3	4	5	6	7	8	9	10	11	12	13	14	15	16	17	18	TOTAL
PAR	4	5	4	4	3	5	3	4	4	4	4	3	4	5	4	4	3	5	**72**
KITE	3	5	4	6	3	4	2	4	5	4	4	2	4	4	4	5	4	5	**72**

HAL SUTTON

THE RIGHT CLUB

⚑

2000 PLAYERS CHAMPIONSHIP

FINAL ROUND

*Hal Sutton is one of only a few professional golfers who can say they were winners in three different
decades. And he didn't just win a few events, either. Sutton won 14 times on the PGA Tour, including the
1983 PGA Championship, his lone major victory. Among all his accomplishments, though, Sutton offers
a single moment that stands out from all the rest, and it happened at the PLAYERS Championship during
the year of the Tiger. It's a moment the entire golf world can recall word for word.*

F ew golfers have a signature moment in their careers. Certainly legends like Jack Nicklaus, Arnold Palmer and
Tiger Woods have a laundry list of them. But the list of other players lucky enough to have just one such moment
is short. Among them is Hal Sutton. His moment hangs on a phrase every golfer knows, and it is one Sutton still
hears every day: "Be the right club. Be the right club today."

"Probably three or four times a day people do that," Sutton said. "That thing has really lasted a long time. It was just a
moment of passion for me."

Sutton uttered the memorable phrase at the 2000 PLAYERS Championship. He had won the event before, but that was
way back in 1983, the same year he won the PGA Championship. It was late March and Sutton was now just a few weeks
away from his 42nd birthday. The PGA Tour was about to be obliterated by a 24-year-old Woods, who would win nine events
that year, including three of the four majors.

Sutton surprised everyone when he shot back-to-back-to-back rounds of 69 to lead the PLAYERS Championship by
one shot over Woods heading into Sunday. Yet even then, no one expected he could hold back a hard-charging Tiger in
the final round.

Hal Sutton eyes his ball at an event during the 2001 PGA Tour season.

"2000 might have been Tiger's greatest year and he had turned everybody away, and now I am the guy who is in front of him . . . That morning when I said my prayers and I was on my knees I realized I wasn't praying to Tiger Woods. I said, 'It'll be all right. He's just a man just like me.' That was the point. They were making him out to be more than a man."

Sutton's belief in himself and commitment to his game paid off in the form of unparalleled consistency to close out the PLAYERS Championship. He played nearly flawless golf in a final round that was broken up over two days because of heavy thunderstorms on Sunday afternoon. He hit 17 of 18 greens and made no bogeys, all while playing alongside Woods. By the end all that stood between Sutton and history was his approach shot at the par-4 18th hole at TPC Sawgrass in Florida. The shot would supply Sutton with the most unforgettable moment of his career.

"When the ball was in the air, I [knew I] had the perfect yardage," Sutton said. "I'd hit the 6-iron exactly the way it was supposed to be hit, and it was headed right at the flag."

But Sutton also knew that anything can take away a great shot — a hard spot on the green or even just a little gust of wind. That's why his legendary phrase came so naturally in the moment with his ball in flight on the 72nd hole just before it hit the green.

"That's just what came out of my mouth," he said. "'Be the right club today.'"

It couldn't have been more right. The ball landed pin-high in the middle of the green, and Sutton let out an impassioned "Yes!" for all to hear. A simple two-putt and he had done it. He'd won his second PLAYERS Championship 17 years after his first — and he'd beaten Woods in the process.

"The second time I won it, against Tiger, that was a whole different sort of win," Sutton said. "That required a deep belief in myself to be able to withstand [the outside pressure] . . . And that took a security inside me not to buy into what everyone else was saying. I had to believe what my heart was telling me."

Sutton's words are advice for all of us, in any walk of life. Believe what your heart is telling you, and be the right club today.

2000 PLAYERS CHAMPIONSHIP **FINAL ROUND**										ROUND 1	ROUND 2	ROUND 3	ROUND 4	TOTAL
										69	69	69	71	**278**
HOLE	1	2	3	4	5	6	7	8	9	10 11 12 13 14 15 16 17 18				TOTAL
PAR	4	5	3	4	4	4	4	3	5	4 5 4 3 4 4 5 3 4				**72**
SUTTON	4	5	3	4	4	4	4	3	5	4 4 4 3 4 4 5 3 4				**71**

BUBBA WATSON

HOOK, LINE AND SINKER

2012 MASTERS TOURNAMENT

FINAL ROUND

Perhaps more so than any other tournament, the Masters is about who roars back on the final nine holes come Sunday. In the fourth round of the 2012 Masters, the drama began early when Louis Oosthuizen made tournament history on the 2nd hole. Then after Bubba Watson forced a playoff on the back nine, it was his turn for some dramatics. With Watson's ball stuck in the trees, his caddie, Ted Scott, saw a little daylight, but it would take a perfect hook to get out. It remains one of the most memorable shots in the history of the game.

The final round of the 2012 Masters started with a bang. Louis Oosthuizen took sole possession of the lead early at −10 when his second shot at the par-5 2nd hole dropped in for an albatross. It was the first albatross on Augusta's 2nd hole and the longest in the tournament's history. His score of 2 instantly dispossessed Peter Hanson and Phil Mickelson of their co-leader status.

Even Bubba Watson, one of many players in hot pursuit of Oosthuizen, couldn't help but admire the shot.

"All I wanted to do was run over and give him a high five," Watson said. "I'm still like a big kid, a fan of the game, and I had a front row seat to history there."

That albatross kicked off a wild finish that saw several players lead or share the lead and a host of others threaten the position.

After bogeying the 1st hole, though, Watson didn't seem to be one of the players most likely to come away from the fray wearing the green jacket. But Watson recalls his caddie, Ted Scott, wanting to make sure the bogey wasn't going to affect his mental approach. "Ted said to me, 'There's a lot of golf. You've already heard roars. You saw Bo Van Pelt shoot a low number. Just keep going, keep going.' I told him, 'I'm still in it. Don't worry. I'm right here.'"

Watson bounced back with a birdie on the 2nd, but that still left him four behind Oosthuizen. Pars on the next two holes and a 35-foot putt for birdie at the 5th got him to two shots back.

Watson continued to play steady golf, posting pars on the next six holes to pull within one shot of Oosthuizen, who faltered with a bogey on the 10th. Watson offset his bogey on 12 with a birdie on 13 but fell to two strokes behind again. The next three holes proved critical.

Watson birdied the 14th. Then at the par-5 15th, he hit a drive straight down the middle and dropped a 7-iron to about 20 feet of the hole. His putt for eagle came up 3 feet short, but Watson converted the birdie and then secured another on 16. He was now 10 under par and tied for the lead. Pars at the 17th and 18th holes sent him and Oosthuizen to a playoff.

Each man made par at the 18th hole to start off. Then at the 10th hole, both hit poor drives that ended up on the right. Oosthuizen had a makeable approach shot, but it landed short of the green. Watson's would be far more difficult.

With his ball in the trees, Watson's options were looking grim. But as he walked down the fairway, Scott had a look and saw an opening.

"Ted said, 'You're good out of the

Bubba Watson tracks his shot from the rough on the 17th hole during the final round of the 2012 Masters.

trees," Watson recalled. "'If you've got a swing, you've got a shot.'"

To convert it, though, Watson would have to make a perfect draw. What came next is one of the most famous shots in the history of the game.

Staring at 160 yards to the hole, give or take, Watson hooked his gap wedge about 40 yards from left to right. It stayed about 15 feet off the ground until it got out from under the trees and then started rising.

When it was done, Watson had left

himself 10 feet for birdie.

Oosthuizen's chip ended up at the back of the green. He made a good effort for par, but his putt didn't drop.

Watson now had two putts for his first green jacket. Safely leaving his first a foot from the hole, he tapped in the second to become the 2012 Masters champion.

"As a golfer, as a fan of the game, winning the Masters and putting on the green jacket is unlike anything else," Watson said. "It was a huge honor."

2012 MASTERS TOURNAMENT
FINAL ROUND

										ROUND 1	ROUND 2	ROUND 3	ROUND 4	TOTAL
										69	71	70	68	**278**

HOLE	1	2	3	4	5	6	7	8	9	10	11	12	13	14	15	16	17	18	TOTAL
PAR	4	5	4	3	4	3	4	5	4	4	4	3	5	4	5	3	4	4	**72**
WATSON	5	4	4	3	3	3	4	5	4	4	4	4	4	3	4	2	4	4	**68**

Davis Love III hugs golfer Zach Johnson after the American side won the Ryder Cup on Sunday, October 2, 2016.

DAVIS LOVE III

O CAPTAIN, MY CAPTAIN

2016 RYDER CUP

SUNDAY SINGLES: REED VS. McILROY

*Davis Love III and his American crew had hammered out their
scheme for the Sunday singles months in advance. But even the best
sometimes second-guess themselves. Lucky for the U.S. side, its captain
went with the instincts that made him a Hall of Famer. He stuck
to the strategy and brought the Ryder Cup back to the States for
the first time in eight years after one of the most iconic showdowns
in the event's history.*

Captain Davis Love III, center, celebrates with his American team after capturing the 2016 Ryder Cup championship.

D avis Love III is a member of the World Golf Hall of Fame with 21 wins on the PGA Tour. Asked recently to name his most memorable, however, Love was unable to narrow it down to just one, or at least the one you'd expect.

"My favorites are the 1997 PGA Championship and the 2016 Ryder Cup," he said. "And as magical as it was to have Jim Nance talking about my dad as I went on to win [the PGA], honestly, I wouldn't trade the '16 Ryder Cup for anything."

Including the PGA Championship isn't surprising. Love won that major, played at the formidable Winged Foot, by five strokes. What made the tournament so memorable for him, however, came afterward.

Love is the son of PGA pro Davis Love Jr., who died in a plane crash almost a decade before his son's win at Winged Foot. After securing the victory, Love made his way up to the 18th hole where, framed by a rainbow, he hugged his caddie, brother Mark, with the memory of their loving dad clearly in mind. It was a moment in golf that will never be forgotten.

"To win at Winged Foot really, really means a lot," Love said. "I feel that the guys that have won there — it's an incredible group to be with. I'm proud to have won on such a great, great golf course."

It was the highlight of his career at the time, one that would be nearly impossible to beat.

Yet nearly two decades later, Love found himself in the midst of another moment etched in golf history. And his part in the drama remains the stuff of legend.

In 2016 Love got his second crack at the Ryder Cup captaincy. That event, held at Hazeltine, is remembered for the defining match of the Sunday singles between Europe's Rory McIlroy and the United States' Patrick Reed. But exactly how this match came to be and why it left such a lasting impression on Love has been shrouded in mystery.

The approach of the modern Ryder Cup on the U.S. side is to keep an open mind and ear to input from the players. Prior iterations had grumbled that they weren't part of the process.

According to Love, he and vice-captains Tiger Woods, Jim Furyk and Tom Lehman all sat down together six months earlier to map out their Sunday singles plan. The group effort was

Patrick Reed of Team USA and Europe's Rory McIlroy shake hands after their Sunday singles round at the 2016 Ryder Cup.

directly tied to what had happened the last time Love was captain, in 2012. In that tournament, the United States led by four strokes heading into the singles but didn't really have a plan. The Americans knew the Europeans were going to do what they always do, which is frontload their side. But the core of the U.S. team was playing so well that they felt they could just roll out anyone in any order and still win.

The Europeans ended up coming back to beat the Americans, and the night afterward European captain Darren Clarke paid a visit to Love in the team room.

"What in the world were you thinking?" he asked Love. "You knew we were going to load the boat."

Love gave his reasons, but Clarke wasn't having any of it.

"That's all BS," he said. "You should have loaded the boat."

Fast-forward to the group meeting in 2016, and all in the room said the best strategy, whether they were up or down coming into Sunday, would be to get on a roll by putting out their best players first. So on Saturday, the night before the singles, the American team already had its plan in place: whoever was playing best would be first out.

After talking with Jordan Spieth and Reed, however, Love began to second-guess himself.

"A couple people came to me on the Saturday night before," Love said. "They heard that Rory was going to be slotted in his typical spot of third or fourth. Jordan Spieth and Patrick Reed heard the same thing, and they came to me and asked to be put out in the third and fourth spots to ensure one of them would get McIlroy."

So Love went back to the room where his vice-captains were filling out the sheet for him. He told them Spieth and Reed wanted to go three and four to ensure one faced McIlroy. They all looked at Love and then each other for a moment.

"No, we already made this decision," they replied. "We made it six months ago. This is what we're doing and we're sticking to our plan."

Love agreed. And good thing he did.

"Sure enough, Rory ends up going out first, instead of third or fourth as we expected," Love said. "And Patrick, who I'm sure wasn't pleased when I initially informed him he was out first, got exactly what he wanted — one of the greatest Ryder Cup matches, if not the greatest Ryder Cup match, of all time."

To say the round was a roller-coaster ride would be an understatement. The first eight holes were perhaps the most intense and dramatic in the long history of the competition, reaching their crescendo at the par-3 8th hole. McIlroy's tee shot settled almost 60 feet from the cup. His unlikely birdie split the hole in two. His celebratory voice was drowned out in a sea of U.S. partisan screams, but the mime of his hand to his ear taunting "I can't hear you!" was heard around the world.

Not to be outdone, Reed faced a 22-foot effort to match McIlroy, and in this delightful theater of the absurd he wouldn't be denied. Reed ignited an even more frenzied response from the faithful that reached a deafening pinnacle when he waved a finger at McIlroy as if to say, "Not in my house!" Such was the current of the match that saw Reed seal the win with yet another birdie putt at the last hole.

Captains can't play for their players, but the decisions they make can be the difference between winning and losing. Love's decision to go with his instincts and trust his vice-captains gave the world one of the most epic head-to-head tilts in golf history.

Henrik Stenson of Sweden looks at his putt on the 9th green during the final round of the 2016 Open.

HENRIK STENSON

STENSON'S HAMMER

2016 OPEN

FINAL ROUND

The 2016 Open showcased a rematch of one of the best head-to-head battles in the event's storied history. On one side was a tireless worker who twice overcame his own demons and, on the other side, a superstar who had cast himself in the role as the ultimate man of the people. On Royal Troon's rugged, unforgiving, unyielding course, Henrik Stenson and Phil Mickelson wowed the crowd once again as they matched each other shot-for-shot in the final round. With the major on the line, it all came down to the par-5 16th.

Henrik Stenson takes in the applause of the gallery after being awarded the Claret Jug for winning the 2016 Open.

by the end of 2011 and a career-low 230th in early 2012.

"The second slump in my career was nothing compared to the one I had in the early 2000s," Stenson said. "So I managed to put my game together with a lot of hard work, a lot of help from my team, and support from my family and friends and everyone else."

Once again, under the watchful eye of Cowen and through his own unyielding work ethic, Stenson's return to form was astounding. He won multiple times in 2013, including the season-long competitions on both the European Tour and PGA Tour with the Race to Dubai and FedEx Cup titles. At The Open at Muirfield, Stenson came close to winning his first major when he finished second to Mickelson. It would be a precursor to their battle at Royal Troon three years later.

At the 2016 Open few expected another showdown between Stenson and Mickelson. Although Stenson had gotten his game back on track yet again, he still hadn't won a major. And since winning The Open in 2013, Mickelson hadn't won, well, anything. But as they did three years earlier,

H enrik Stenson epitomizes his Viking heritage.

A strong and tall Swede, he slams into the ball seemingly with the velocity of Thor's hammer. But his road to becoming one of the best wasn't a linear path of ascent. Early in his pro career, and after having already won on the European Tour in 2001, Stenson suddenly lost his swing. Forget about hitting a fairway . . .

"He couldn't hit the earth," said his longtime coach Pete Cowen.

The process of rebuilding his swing, game and psyche took Stenson and Cowen over two years to complete. But once they did, Stenson got back on track with multiple victories from 2005 to 2008 and eventually reached fourth in the world rankings. Then in 2009 he hit his competitive zenith when he won the PLAYERS Championship.

Soon afterward, however, another competitive valley followed. Stenson dropped to 207th in the rankings

FINAL ROUND

										ROUND 1	ROUND 2		ROUND 3		ROUND 4					TOTAL
										68	65		68		63					**264**
HOLE	1	2	3	4	5	6	7	8	9	10	11	12	13	14	15	16	17	18		**TOTAL**
PAR	4	4	4	5	3	5	4	3	4	4	4	4	4	3	4	5	3	4		**71**
STENSON	5	3	3	4	3	4	4	2	4	3	5	4	4	2	3	4	3	3		**63**

the two put on a show at Royal Troon Golf Club in Ayrshire, Scotland, in what many regard as one of the greatest head-to-head duels ever in a final round.

Through three rounds Stenson and Mickelson had separated themselves from the rest of the field. With the next closest player five shots back, it would be a two-horse race the rest of the way.

Mickelson, sitting one shot behind Stenson, sent an early message with a birdie on the 1st hole, while Stenson struggled to a bogey. Just like that, Mickelson now had the lead.

"That wasn't the start I was looking for, but more important was what I did afterward," Stenson said. "I was sticking to my plan and committing to my shots, and that got me straight back in the ballgame with two quick birdies on 2 and 3."

Those birdies saw Stenson retake the lead. Mickelson came back right away at the 4th with an eagle, but a birdie by Stenson had them tied once more. After both parred the 5th, birdies by each man kept them knotted until Stenson broke the logjam at the famed 8th hole, the par-3 Postage Stamp. There Stenson made a birdie to reach

−16, but he was still clinging to a one-stroke lead.

"I knew he was going to be there and pushing me all the way," Stenson said. "I just tried to stick to my game plan, play the best I could and put the best score together that I could."

Both men birdied the 10th before Stenson's three-putt bogey at the 11th dropped him back into a tie. The battle continued through 12 and 13 as each made par.

At the 14th and 15th holes, Stenson made his move by dropping a pair of aggressive birdie putts.

"It was a 20-footer [on 14], and I just thought, 'How many chances coming in here am I going to have to try to pull away?' Because I knew he wasn't going to make too many mistakes by the looks of it, so I just knew I had to take it," Stenson said. "Those two putts [on 14 and 15] were the ones that pulled me ahead and put me two in front."

At the par-5 16th, Mickelson faced a makeable eagle attempt while Stenson had work to do to make a birdie. A Mickelson make and Stenson miss would be a massive swing.

Mickelson's eagle putt looked like

it was going to go in, but it just snuck by the hole. That left Stenson standing over a 5-footer downhill to keep it a two-shot lead.

"That was a very important putt to make," Stenson said, "and probably the most pressure I felt all day."

But two-stroke leads in The Open are tenuous, at best. And the par-3 17th stood ready to derail Stenson's first win at a major.

"It's one of the harder holes on the golf course," Stenson said. "I just knew I had to hit a good shot and hit the green and not make worse than 3 there."

Stenson closed like a champion. After securing par on 17 he hammered his second shot toward the flag on 18 on his way to another birdie, his 10th of the round, finishing three strokes ahead of Mickelson.

Stenson had shot a 63 to reach a record −20, the lowest score in a major championship. He also tied Johnny Miller for the best final round ever in a major.

"I felt like that week was going to be my turn," Stenson said. "I think that was the extra self-belief that made me go all the way that week."

Jordan Spieth celebrates a birdie on the 16th hole during the final round of the 2017 Open.

JORDAN SPIETH

EAGLE-EYED

⚑

2017 OPEN

FINAL ROUND

*The 2017 Open had everything: wild weather, wild shots, clamoring
fans and excited broadcasters. At the center of it all was Jordan Spieth.
But this wouldn't be an easy march to victory. Spieth would have
to battle the elements, fight through the pressure and hold back
Matt Kuchar if he was to win The Open for the first time.
A bogey — and one of the savviest uses of rules the sport has seen
in some time — turned things around for Spieth. But it was an
epic eagle that sealed the deal.*

Jordan Spieth carefully weighs his options for a drop as he plays the 13th hole during the final round of the 2017 Open.

The 2017 Open Championship was hosted at Royal Birkdale Golf Club in Southport, England. It's one of the world's great links courses. In fact, many believe Royal Birkdale is the best among The Open's list of courses, if not the best course in the world.

Scoring that year was a reflection of the weather, and luckily for the players the tournament started in good conditions. Jordan Spieth, Matt Kuchar and Brooks Koepka all took advantage of light early-morning rain and afternoon sun to post rounds of 65 and share the lead at –5.

On Friday, however, the weather turned windy and foul, and the scoring followed in kind. Only eight players posted sub-70 scores that day. Koepka and Kuchar weren't among them, although their rounds of 72 and

71, respectively, were solid, all things considered. Spieth, meanwhile, shot 69 to stand alone atop the leaderboard at –6, two shots clear of Kuchar.

The third round brought with it sunshine and good scoring once more. Spieth matched his opening-round 65 and now stood at –11, three clear of Kuchar.

Sunday was a pretty day with only a chance of occasional passing showers, so the golf world came into the final round believing Spieth would continue his steady form. But Spieth seemed nervy and fidgety from the get-go. He pulled his opening drive slightly and ended up in an extremely unlucky spot. His ball kicked off the top of a dune and settled in thick rough, below his stance. After a bogey, his lead was down to two strokes over Kuchar.

On the 2nd hole, a Spieth par and a

Kuchar birdie saw the lead cut to one. Both bogeyed the 3rd hole, and on the 4th Spieth continued his rocky start with his third bogey in the opening four holes. Suddenly his three-shot lead was gone.

"I was questioning why I couldn't just perform the shots that I was before," Spieth said. "And sometimes you just can't really figure it out or put your finger on it."

Spieth appeared to steady the ship with a birdie at the 5th hole. After Kuchar bogeyed the 6th, Spieth had clawed back in front by two strokes once more. But another birdie–bogey exchange at the 9th hole leveled the lead again. Both men stood at –8 as they made the turn.

Spieth and Kuchar parred holes 10, 11 and 12. As they climbed the hill to the 13th tee box, the boisterous gallery

2017 OPEN **FINAL ROUND**										ROUND 1 65	ROUND 2 69	ROUND 3 65	ROUND 4 69	TOTAL **268**
HOLE	1	2	3	4	5	6	7	8	9	10 11	12 13	14 15	16 17 18	TOTAL
PAR	4	4	4	3	4	4	3	4	4	4 4	3 4	3 5	4 5 4	**70**
SPIETH	5	4	5	4	3	4	3	4	5	4 4	3 5	2 3	3 4 4	**69**

was pressing the rope line so much that players, caddies, officials and the rest could only thread their way through the crowd one at a time. It had also started to rain, and the wind was blowing slightly into the players. With all the distractions, Spieth pushed his tee shot way right of the fairway from the elevated tee box.

"My reaction when I looked up was, 'Oh, wow, I don't even know what's over there,'" Spieth said.

The ball had struck a spectator and ricocheted onto a dune that was a gnarly tangle of grass and hay. That position forced Spieth to declare his ball unplayable, which afforded him a drop. He had three choices: go back to the tee box and try again, drop within two club lengths of where the ball lay but no closer to the hole, or drop as far back as he wanted provided it was on line with the flagstick. This last option is the one he chose. But it wasn't so straightforward. As he told reporters after the round was finished, "I just asked the question, 'Is the driving range out of bounds?' And I got the answer, 'No.'"

But moving back to the driving range meant Spieth then had to deal with equipment trucks that were parked along the far side of the range for the tournament. Under tournament rules, those trucks were temporarily immovable objects, and that granted Spieth line of sight — so he was able to drop his ball in a far better position.

With that, Spieth was able to pull himself from the brink of disaster with a 3-iron to the front right of a greenside pot bunker. From there he made a gutsy up and down for bogey from a tight lie that sloped away to a short-sided pin.

Even though the bogey dropped him out of the lead, it was a turning point in his round. (Spieth has since sent the 3-iron to Royal Birkdale to be displayed.)

Spieth seemed renewed by his savvy rule reading and gutsy shot, and he nearly made a hole in one with his 6-iron tee shot at the 14th hole. It settled about 5 feet from the cup for an easy birdie. With Kuchar's par they were once again tied atop the leaderboard.

"The shot on 14 was the best shot I've probably ever hit in a major

championship given the situation," Spieth said.

Spieth continued to hit good shots, with two more at the par-5 15th hole leaving him a 48-footer for a chance at eagle. Spieth lined it up and struck it. The shot was captured live by European Tour player-turned-broadcaster Paul Eales, who let out a golf-themed version of famous World Cup announcer Andres Cantor's "Gooooooooooaaal!" when Spieth drained the eagle putt. That gave Spieth a one-shot edge over Kuchar, who made birdie there himself.

Momentum is a powerful thing in sports, and Spieth kept rolling. At the 16th hole he made yet another birdie, this time across the width of the green. His lead was now two strokes.

Both players birdied the 17th hole, leaving Spieth with a comfortable two-shot lead at the 18th. He made par there for a three-shot victory over Kuchar, who finished with a bogey.

As unlikely as it is that a bogey could trigger a rally, the last six holes at The Open at Royal Birkdale in 2017 produced as amazing a stretch of golf as any in the sport's history.

Republic of Ireland's
Shane Lowry celebrates
with Claret Jug after
winning The 2019 Open
Championship at Royal
Portrush Golf Club.

SHANE LOWRY

ONE FOR THE IRISH

2019 OPEN

FINAL ROUND

In the realm of golf, Shane Lowry's journey at the 2019 Open in Royal Portrush, Northern Ireland, was a tale for the ages. As he triumphantly held the Claret Jug amidst the rolling green landscapes of his beloved Ireland, tears of joy streamed down his face. It was a moment that not only defined a remarkable tournament but also resonated deeply with the hearts of the Irish, celebrating what felt like a national victory.

Shane Lowry celebrates his birdie on the 15th hole during Round 4 of the 2019 Open Championship at Royal Portrush Golf Club.

G olf has an uncanny way of delivering the perfect story at the perfect time. Consider the 2019 Open at Royal Portrush in Northern Ireland. The last time The Open was contested on the island was at Royal Portrush in 1951. When Irishman Shane Lowry hoisted the Claret Jug amid the jubilation of the tear-streaked faithful, you cannot deny the storyline's perfection.

"Oh, my God. It was amazing," said Lowry in the wake of his victory. "It's hard to believe. It's just hard to believe. And it was just — it was great out there today. It's funny, I sometimes struggle to play in front of the home crowd, but not over the last few days. I played lovely. It's obviously very nice. It was just incredible to walk down 18. The crowd was going wild. Singing olé, olé, olé. It's like something that — I just couldn't believe it was happening to me. And obviously to have all my

friends and family there. I spotted my family when I walked around the corner to have a look where the flag was, and I spotted them all at the back of the green. To be honest, I welled up a little bit and Bo [Martin, my caddie] told me to catch a hold of myself, I still had to hit a shot. Thankfully I hit a decent shot in there and two-putted."

The feeling at Royal Portrush was more than just the euphoria that accompanies a victory, even that of a breakthrough maiden major and a dominating performance. This was different. It was a cathartic moment of overcoming personal fears and insecurities.

"I was quite nervous and anxious Wednesday evening. You come up here and the last thing you want to do is miss the cut. That's the last thing you want to do. And that was kind of in my mind. I wanted to play at least four days and wanted to put up a

good show for myself. Being in home. I was showing good form over the last while."

This was about more than just performing well on Irish soil. In 2016 at the U.S. Open at Oakmont, Lowry would surrender a four-shot, 54-hole lead to Dustin Johnson — the exact lead he possessed at Royal Portrush. At the Open at Carnoustie two years later, Lowry failed to survive the halfway cut. "I sat in the car park in Carnoustie, almost a year ago right to this week, and I cried. I didn't want to carry on; golf wasn't my friend at the time. It was something that had become very stressful, and it was weighing on me and I just didn't like doing it. And look what a difference a year makes, I suppose."

In an individual sport like golf, it is amazing how often players admit that they cannot not do it alone. Regarding his battle against self-doubt, Lowry refers to a cup of coffee with his coach Neil Manchip the day before the tournament and how the support of those around him all contributed to his triumph: "So, yeah, it really settled me down. I said after that — well, I left, and I really felt like I could go out and perform to the best of my ability the next day. So, it obviously helped me an awful lot along the way. I suppose I didn't even know going out this Sunday

2019 OPEN FINAL ROUND										ROUND 1	ROUND 2		ROUND 3		ROUND 4		TOTAL	
										67	67		63		72		**269**	
HOLE	1	2	3	4	5	6	7	8	9	10	11	12	13	14	15	16	17	18	TOTAL
PAR	4	5	3	4	4	3	5	4	4	4	4	5	3	4	4	3	4	4	**71**
LOWRY	5	5	3	3	3	3	4	5	5	4	5	5	3	5	3	3	4	4	**72**

morning if I was good enough to win a major. I knew I was able to put a few days together. I knew I was able to play the golf course. I just went out there and tried to give my best. And look, I'm here now, a major champion. I can't believe I'm saying it, to be honest. I think the people around me really believed that I could, which helped me an awful lot. I do remember a lot of times in the past when I'm down on myself and serious chats with Neil, he always reminded me, he always said that I was going to win one, at least one, he said. So, I suppose when the people around you really believe in you, it helps you an awful lot."

Basking in the warmth of accomplishment, Lowry shared that even though he was coming off a third-round score of 63 in which he broke the course record and set a new 54-hole record at The Open, standing on the tee on Sunday was something different entirely.

"Obviously I had a nice healthy lead going out and I hit a ropy tee shot on the first. I hit actually a decent second shot, but it didn't go as far as I thought it was going to go. Now, I'm standing on the first green, Tommy has a great chance of birdie and I'm putting for bogey from eight feet. There's a potential three-shot swing. He misses, I make, and there's only one shot. That settled me an awful lot."

Lowry would make birdies at the fourth, fifth and seventh holes, gaining a six-shot lead on Fleetwood, but bogies on the eighth and ninth as foul weather rolled in and required more focus.

"Around the turn, I had a look at a few leaderboards, and it was so hard out there. When that big shower came in on the eighth, the ninth tee shot was just like put the ball down and hope for the best because it was incredible, the rain that was coming down so hard. Then I think when I finally started to feel comfortable was after 14. I had a lovely one on 13. Tommy had missed the green and I hit a bad tee shot there. It was a silly bad tee shot. It was an easy 9-iron downwind, should be hitting the green with that. To get that opening and make par, that was huge. To be honest, I played the last five holes even par, even though I bogeyed 14, I thought I played the last five holes incredibly well. And I felt incredibly good. I felt like I was

going to do it, especially after 14 when Tommy went double, I went bogey. But I went five ahead with four to play."

At the short and quirky par 4, 17th, Lowry could finally start to enjoy his labors.

"When I hit my tee shot on 17, that was it. It was then I started to enjoy it. I didn't really let myself think about it until I hit my tee shot on 17. As soon as I hit that tee shot, I knew that I couldn't really lose a ball from there, and that's how I felt. So it's an incredible feeling."

The unique way the R&A allows the gallery to flood onto the 18th fairway on the final hole always leaves an indelible image, but on this day, it meant so much more: from Dublin to Belfast, Irish hearts rejoiced in unison.

"To be honest, like, I walked down there, and I tried to soak it in as much as I could. It was hard to soak it in because it's very surreal. It's a very surreal experience going down there. Especially with, I'm sure there was a lot of the crowd that wanted me to win today. So, it was quite surreal, yeah. I'm Irish. I grew up holing putts back home to win The Open. It was always The Open."

Once again, golf delivered.

Phil Mickelson after a missed putt on the 11th green during the final round at the PGA Championship.

PHIL MICKELSON

NO DOUBT

2021 PGA CHAMPIONSHIP

FINAL ROUND

Doubt loomed large for Phil Mickelson as he entered the 103rd PGA Championship in 2021. Ranked 115th globally, he hadn't seen a top-10 finish in 17 attempts on the PGA Tour, nor in any major since 2016. Approaching his 51st birthday, he faced the twin specters of age and underperformance. Yet, this was Phil Mickelson — a legend known for defying the odds. His journey to rewrite history began that week.

Phil Mickelson holds the Wanamaker Trophy after winning the PGA Championship golf tournament on the Ocean Course.

 "Although I believed it, until I actually did it, there was a lot of doubt, I'm sure."

Sometimes doubt is justified, even for a legend like Phil Mickelson. He came into the 103rd PGA Championship at Kiawah in 2021 as the 115th ranked player in the world. He was in the midst of an 0-for-17 stretch without a top-10 finish on the PGA Tour, with no top-10's in any majors since The Open in 2016. What's more, ol' Phil was only one month shy of his 51st birthday. So, working against him that week was his world ranking, a stretch of bad play and Father Time. Not the best circumstances to get into a positive mind set — but then again, there are few minds like Phil's.

"I believed for a long time that I could play at this level again. I didn't see why I couldn't, but I wasn't executing the way I believed I could, and with the help of a lot of people, my wife especially, [coach] Andrew Getson and my brother Tim and [agent] Steve Loy, I've been able to make progress and have this week," the World Golf Hall of Fame member recounted in the wake of his history-making victory that week.

The five-time major champion knew that winning a sixth major at an age when he could join the AARP would be something no one else had done in the history of the sport. Since the first major, The Open, in 1860, no one over 50 had ever won one of golf's most coveted prizes. But this is Phil. Often referred to as the "smartest guy in the room" by both admirers and detractors, Mickelson has never shied from employing his intellect, charisma and massive talent to work magic with a golf ball, to build a commercial endorsement empire or to sell the narrative that he is unequaled. But sometimes it seemed like the man who had accomplished so much would get in his own way. This major was different.

"I tried to stay more in the present and at the shot at hand and not jump ahead and race," Phil explained. "I tried to shut my mind to a lot of stuff going around. I wasn't watching TV. I wasn't getting on my phone. I was just trying to quiet things down because I'll get my thoughts racing, and I really just tried to stay calm."

Mickelson's start to the championship looked like a continuation of the way he had been playing. He made four bogeys over his first six holes, but on the back nine he showed signs of life with four birdies. Mickelson grew

FINAL ROUND

										ROUND 1	ROUND 2		ROUND 3		ROUND 4		TOTAL
										70	69		70		73		**282**
HOLE	1	2	3	4	5	6	7	8	9	10	11	12	13	14	15	16	17	18	TOTAL
PAR	4	5	4	4	3	4	5	3	4	4	5	4	4	3	4	5	3	4	**72**
MICKELSON	5	4	5	4	2	5	4	3	4	3	5	4	5	4	4	4	4	4	**73**

stronger over the next two rounds until a double-bogey on the 13th in the third round saw his lead cut to only one stroke over Brooks Koepka heading into Sunday. Mickelson's lead was lost immediately in the final round with a bogey at the first, and birdie by Koepka saw a two-stroke swing. Now, the hunted became the hunter: Koepka stumbling to a double-bogey on the second hole against Mickelson's birdie seemed to suggest Mickelson might be in for a punch-counter-punch affair like he had against Henrik Stenson at Royal Troon — the last time he factored in a major. But Mickelson's march to glory seemed to stall despite a hole-out for birdie at the fifth hole. Enter his brother and caddy, Tim, to right the ship at the perfect time.

"I'll tell you a perfect example, and this is an intangible that makes him relatable or to understand me, get the best out of me and makes him a great caddie is. I'm walking off six, I had made some uncommitted swings the first six holes. I had been striking the ball awesome the first three days. I had a wonderful warm up session, like I was ready to go and I made

some uncommitted swings the first six holes. He pulled me aside and said, 'If you're going to win this thing, you're going to have to make committed golf swings.' It hit me in the head, I can't make passive — I can't control the outcome, I have to swing committed. The first one I made was the drive on seven. Good drive on seven gave me a chance to get down by the green and make birdie. From there on, I hit a lot of really good shots because I was committed to each one."

Mickelson would go out in level par and hold a two-shot edge over Koepka and Louis Oostuizen at the turn.

"I hit a couple of good shots on the back. I thought the 7-iron into 10 was really good because I had to start that ball out over the bunker at the bunker's edge and made that birdie putt there. So that was a big swing."

Mickelson would enjoy a four-shot lead at this point, but his margin would narrow after finding water at the 13th that resulted in bogey. He would post another at the 14th and see his lead cut in half before settling down over the next two holes.

"I made some good tee shots on 15 and 16. Those were really good

swings," Mickelson recalls. In fact, his drive at the 16th was 366 yards, the longest on that hole for the championship. A bogey at the 17th paved his triumphant walk down the 18th, where he was surrounded by a rapturous gallery that engulfed him until he gloriously emerged as the people's champion.

"I've never had that experience, and to see that kind of — to feel that kind of excitement and enthusiasm was — and be at the forefront of that was pretty special. That's a moment I'll always, always cherish."

Mickelson would post a 1-over 73 to finish on 6 under par, two shots clear of Koepka and Oosthuizen. He recorded his sixth major championship and became the oldest major champion of all time, bettering the record Julius Burrows set in 1968 when he won the PGA Championship at the age of 48.

"I hope that this inspires some to just put in that little extra work, because first of all, there's no reason why you can't accomplish your goals at an older age. It just takes a little more work."

There's no one like ol' Phil.

GREAT COMEBACKS

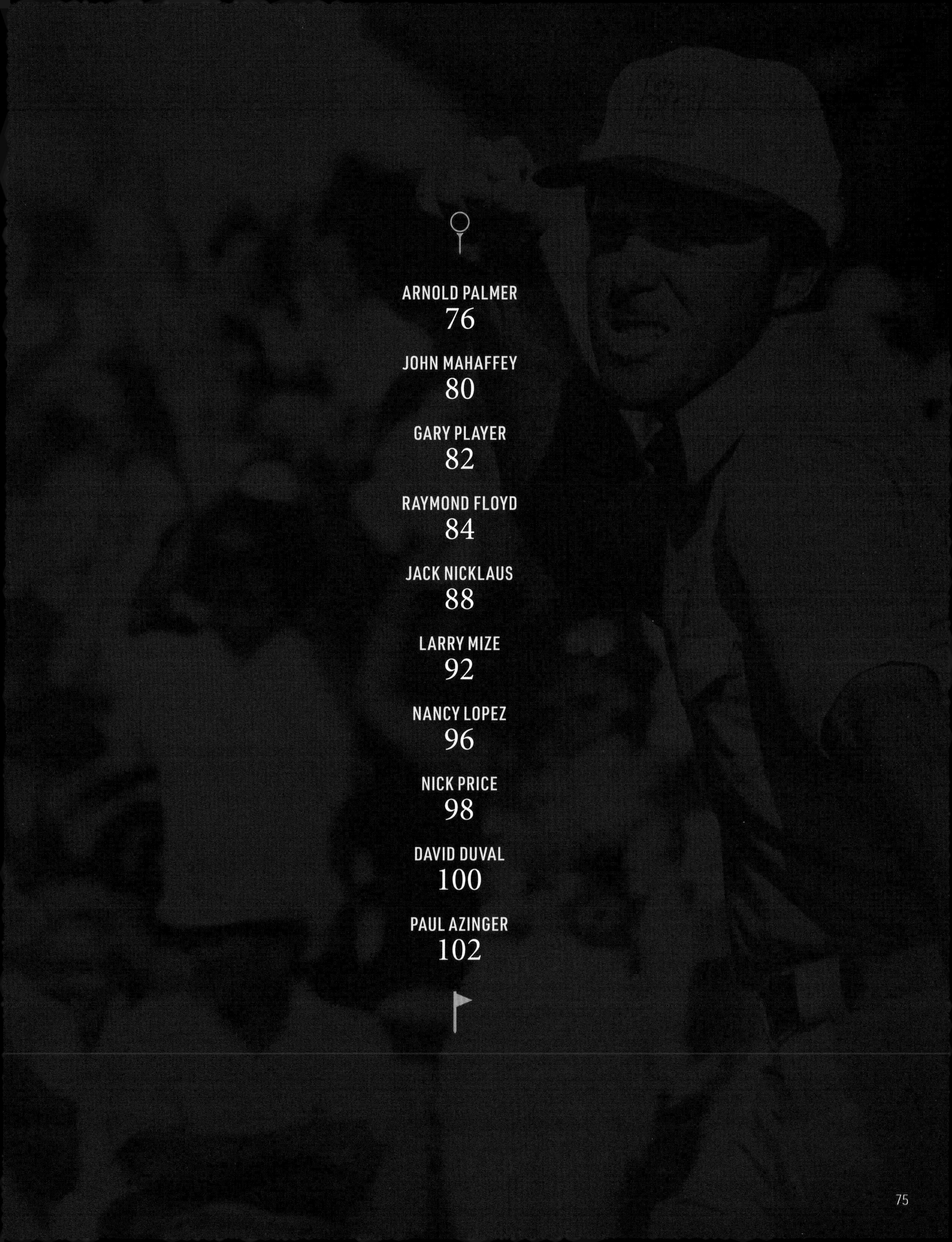

ARNOLD PALMER
76

JOHN MAHAFFEY
80

GARY PLAYER
82

RAYMOND FLOYD
84

JACK NICKLAUS
88

LARRY MIZE
92

NANCY LOPEZ
96

NICK PRICE
98

DAVID DUVAL
100

PAUL AZINGER
102

Arnold Palmer throws his visor into the air after his comeback victory at the 1960 U.S. Open.

ARNOLD PALMER

LONG LIVE THE KING

⚑

1960 U.S. OPEN

FINAL ROUND

Arnold Palmer's dominance is well documented. He is the owner of 62 PGA Tour victories and in his career he won seven majors. His spectacular play at the Masters may define his legacy, but winning his only U.S. Open is widely regarded as his crowning moment. In 1960 he beat out both a young prodigy and a golfing legend down the stretch to pull out the victory. And after a comeback for the ages, "the King" was officially anointed.

Arnold Palmer's prowess at the Masters is well chronicled. Four of his seven career majors came at Augusta, and it was there that his fearless, go-for-broke style of attacking a golf course was displayed in all its raging glory. Among all his Hall of Fame achievements, however, the 1960 U.S. Open stands out. Palmer had already won four other events that year, including the Masters, and came into the tournament with his confidence at an all-time high.

"This U.S. Open had a different feel to it," he said. "My desire to go out and play Cherry Hills was intense."

Cherry Hills sat alongside the Rocky Mountains just outside Denver, Colorado. With the course that far above sea level, he knew the ball would carry a long way.

But things didn't start so well for Palmer.

On the very first hole, a 346-yard par 4, Palmer pushed his tee shot into a ditch and posted a tournament-opening double-bogey on his way to a first-round score of 72.

Arnold Palmer, left, poses for photos following his only U.S. Open victory. In the center is a young Jack Nicklaus.

Undaunted, Palmer attempted to drive the green on the opening hole in his second and third rounds as well. But he missed the mark again on both occasions and finished with scores of 71 and 72. Through three rounds he found himself mired in 15th place.

Sitting seven shots back of the lead, Palmer's repeated attempts to drive the first green had proved costly. But the same hole, same shot would play a dramatic role come Saturday afternoon (U.S. Opens were played with 36 holes on Saturday in those days as opposed to 18 holes on both Saturday and Sunday) as Palmer staged what many call the greatest comeback in U.S. Open history.

Between the morning and afternoon rounds on Saturday, Palmer sat eating a cheeseburger and drinking ice tea with Ken Venturi and Bob Rosburg, along with writers Bob Drum and Dan Jenkins. According to several sources the conversation went something like this:

"I might shoot 65," Palmer said. "What would that do?"

"Nothing," Drum harrumphed. "You're too far back."

"It would give me 280. Doesn't 280 always win the Open?" Palmer reasoned.

"Yeah," chuckled Drum. "When [Ben] Hogan shoots it . . . You're too far back."

With that, an angry Palmer marched from the table.

"That set a fire off inside me," Palmer said. "I was pretty mad."

Standing on the first tee, Palmer faced the same decision he had in his first three rounds: go for the green or play it safe? Anyone who knows anything about Palmer would tell you there was little debate. The fact that he was seven shots back only furthered his resolve.

"I knew I could drive that green," he said, "and I had gone for it in every round."

This time his persimmon driver delivered a crushing blow that sent the ball rocketing on a perfect trajectory. Bouncing through a belt of rough, the ball slowed just enough to settle on the green, 20 feet from the hole.

"I heard a loud cheer from the gallery around the green," Palmer said. "Walking off the tee I felt a powerful surge of adrenaline."

After his eagle putt barely crept past the edge of the hole, Palmer converted for the birdie and added another on the next hole. A close wedge shot on the 3rd hole nailed down another birdie, and a 20-foot putt on the 4th gave him yet another. He was now just three shots back.

"I knew I was on a roll," he said.

1960 U.S. OPEN										ROUND 1		ROUND 2		ROUND 3		ROUND 4		TOTAL
FINAL ROUND										72		71		72		65		**280**
HOLE	1	2	3	4	5	6	7	8	9	10	11	12	13	14	15	16	17	18	TOTAL
PAR	4	4	4	4	5	3	4	3	4	4	5	3	4	4	3	4	5	4	**71**
PALMER	3	3	3	3	5	2	3	4	4	4	4	3	4	4	3	4	5	4	**65**

Surprisingly Palmer only parred the short par-5 5th hole after greenside bunkering his second shot with a 3-wood. On the 6th hole, however, a 7-iron put him back on the birdie train, and he followed that up with another on the 7th. Through the first seven holes he had made six birdies.

"Some of the shots I hit are constant memories," he said, "even today."

A bogey on the 8th hole did nothing to deflate his confidence. He'd jammed himself back into contention.

As he approached the 9th hole, Palmer spotted Drum in the crowd.

"I said to Bob, 'Well, well, what are you doing here since I have no chance?'"

Palmer parred the hole to complete his front side.

Meanwhile, a 20-year-old amateur named Jack Nicklaus, who was paired with 47-year-old Hogan, held the tournament lead at 5 under par. Nicklaus was one ahead of the 30-year-old Palmer and a host of other contenders, including Hogan. As amazing as Palmer's front-nine score of 30 was, the young Nicklaus had cruised through with a highly respectable 32.

It's easy to record the score, comment on its brilliance and then assume Palmer tore through the competition with the same magnitude he did the golf course in that final round. But Nicklaus' performance and Hogan's gritty determination meant the three were ready to duke it out down the stretch. As is normally the case at a U.S. Open, it came down to who had better control of his nerves.

Nicklaus was the first to break. On the 13th hole, with 3 feet left to save par and maintain a one-stroke lead, he noticed a poorly repaired ball mark in his path. Perhaps in awe and slightly intimidated by Hogan, the young amateur failed to ask the great champion if he agreed the mark needed further tending. Instead Nicklaus decided to putt through it, and the mini-crater redirected the ball's path just enough to spin it out of the hole, resulting in a bogey. He followed that up by three-putting the 14th hole.

Then it was Hogan's turn to crack. By the time he reached the final two holes, he had hit 34 of 34 greens through the day's play. Perhaps buoyed by his success, he attempted risky shots to reach the green on both 17 and 18. Each ended up in the water, clearing the way for Palmer to take control.

"I was aware, as much as you could be, of what was going on around me," Palmer said. "But mostly I was focusing on my game."

Having witnessed Nicklaus and Hogan fall away, Palmer employed a conservative strategy and cruised home with the championship in hand. He finished two strokes in front of Nicklaus (who finished second), while Hogan finished ninth.

The significance of three of the greatest golfers of all time converging in this major wasn't lost on those chronicling the game at that time. Sports Illustrated's Dan Jenkins wrote that "on that afternoon in the span of just 18 holes, we witnessed the arrival of Nicklaus, the coronation of Palmer and the end of Hogan."

The victory was a massive boost to Palmer's surging dominance and popularity. His 65 in the final round set a championship record, and his comeback from seven shots back is a record that still stands.

"To say I was happy with that U.S. Open win would be an understatement," he said.

JOHN MAHAFFEY
IT HAPPENED IN SUDDEN DEATH

1978 PGA CHAMPIONSHIP

PLAYOFF

John Mahaffey learned how to play from the Ben Hogan manual. He idolized the legend growing up, so when Hogan took his fellow Texan under his wing, it was a dream come true for Mahaffey. For much of his four decades on the PGA Tour, Mahaffey was mentored by Hogan, and the two became close friends. Mahaffey won 10 times on the Tour, none sweeter than the 1978 PGA Championship, his only victory at a major. It came in dramatic fashion, in a sudden-death three-way playoff. And after it was all over, congratulations were in order from his mentor and friend.

John Mahaffey was born in Texas and played golf collegiately at the University of Houston, where he won the 1970 NCAA championships. Being a Texan, Mahaffey looked up to none other than Ben Hogan.

"He was a hero growing up. I learned how to play out of Ben Hogan's book," he said. "I really didn't have any formal teaching."

Mahaffey turned pro in 1971, and by the 1978 PGA Tour season, he had played in well over 100 events, amassing more than 40 top 10s and 10 runner-up finishes. Mahaffey had also cut his teeth in 14 major championships, making the top 10 in four of them, including a second-place finish at the 1976 U.S. Open. During that time he met and got to know Hogan.

"We struck up a tremendous friendship," Mahaffey said. "He was my mentor for almost 20 years and I learned a lot from him — not lesson-wise, just how to approach the game, how to attack a golf course. He was probably one of the best at course management I have ever seen."

That friendship and Hogan's wisdom would come in handy for the 1978 PGA Championship at Oakmont Country Club in Pennsylvania.

The most challenging part of Oakmont is always its greens, which can be treacherous. Mahaffey's putting did him no favors

John Mahaffey is all smiles as he holds onto the PGA Championship trophy after his playoff victory in 1978.

Over the final holes the lead ping-ponged between Watson, Mahaffey and Jerry Pate. When Pate missed a par putt at the last for the win, all three had finished 8 under par. A sudden-death playoff would determine the PGA Champion.

They began on the long 469-yard par-4 1st hole, a tough one to birdie. It was a par for all three men and on they went. Mahaffey's moment would come on the second playoff hole.

Mahaffey hit a 3-wood off the tee and killed it down the left side. His 9-iron onto the green landed just left and finished pin-high 12 feet away. Pate ended up in the rough and took three shots to get to the green, while Watson missed his birdie attempt. That left the door open for Mahaffey. But Oakmont's greens, even after having been softened, were still speedy, and Mahaffey knew it wouldn't come easy.

"One of the fastest putts in the world," Mahaffey recalled of the birdie putt. "That one was down-grain, downhill and just fast as greased lightning. It went right in the center, and I just barely touched it."

With that birdie Mahaffey had collected his only major championship.

"That was probably the putt of my life."

in the opening round, however, as he struggled out of the gates with a 75. If he was to get back in the mix, he'd need to figure something out — "in the dirt," as Hogan would say.

"Opening with a 75 like I did, I went to the practice tee . . . and I spent the [rest of the] day there until dark," Mahaffey said. "I thought I found something that would work. It was an alignment issue, and I started aiming a little bit left, à la Trevino."

With his game back in order, Mahaffey shot 67 and 68 in the second and third rounds. Yet even with those two solid scores, he still started the final round seven shots behind the leader, Tom Watson. Mahaffey quickly found his stride, though, and his putting would be key to his comeback.

Rain during the week had softened the greens, and it was a warm August day, good for scoring. Mahaffey made birdie putts from 15, 35 and 12 feet on the front nine. Then he started his back nine with a 50-foot bomb on the 10th hole. At the same time, Watson was taking a double-bogey. "I made [the] unbelievable putt on number 10," Mahaffey said. "And when Tom took a double-bogey, that was a swing of three shots." Mahaffey then made a 25-footer on the 11th that put him right in the mix. "I began to think I could win," he recalled. By the 13th hole, they were tied for the lead.

1978 PGA CHAMPIONSHIP

ROUND 1	ROUND 2	ROUND 3	ROUND 4	TOTAL
75	67	68	66	**276**

PLAYOFF

HOLE	1	2	TO PAR
PAR	4	4	
MAHAFFEY	4	3	**−1**
WATSON	4	4	E
PATE	4	4	E

GARY PLAYER

THE IMPOSSIBLE COMEBACK

1978 MASTERS TOURNAMENT

FINAL ROUND

Gary Player won over 165 professional golf tournaments, 24 of them on the PGA Tour. Born in South Africa, he won 63 times on the country's pro tour and remains its all-time record holder. Over the course of his PGA career he won nine major championships, but his last and possibly most impressive major was his 1978 Masters triumph. That year "the Black Knight" pulled off one of the greatest comebacks in PGA Tour history.

Gary Player is one of the greatest golfers who ever lived. He was inducted into the World Golf Hall of Fame in 1974, and in 2012 he was honored with the PGA Tour Lifetime Achievement Award. He was also a fitness pioneer, recognized as one of the first pro golfers to make health and wellness a part of his regular routine, earning him the nickname "Mr. Fitness."

But the name you probably know him better by is "the Black Knight." And in 1978 Player earned that nickname when he slew the entire field at Augusta in just nine holes.

Coming into Augusta that year, Player was 42 years old and the wins were declining. He'd already played in the Masters 20 times, winning the green jacket twice (1961 and 1974). But all that experience didn't alter his perspective as he strolled along the dramatic entrance to the clubhouse at Augusta National Golf Club.

"I like to always walk through Magnolia Lane, just take about five minutes to realize how lucky I am and how I appreciate things in life," Player said. "I think gratitude is an essential ingredient in life."

Player's experience at Augusta came in handy, as he hung around just close enough in the first three rounds to remain within striking distance. With rounds of 72, 72 and 69, he was 3 under par and seven shots back prior to the final round. It was then that Player remembered a conversation he had with his 14-year-old son.

"He said, 'Dad you are playing so well you could shoot 65 and win the tournament,'" Player recalled. "Well, I did play well."

Since Player was so far back, he began his round almost 40 minutes before the final group. His front nine started slowly, and when he got to the 9th tee he was only 4 under for the tournament. That was where arguably the greatest final round in major championship history began.

Player birdied the 9th hole, then hit a 5-iron onto the 10th green and made a 25-foot birdie to take him to −6. All of a sudden his momentum was building. For the par-3 12th hole, Player hit a 7-iron to 15 feet, which led to another birdie. On the par-5 13th, his 4-iron onto the green led to an easy two-putt birdie.

The putter had come alive. And just like that, Player was now 8 under.

His birdie on the par-5 15th hole that came in the form of two putts from 80 feet took him to 9 under. And another birdie on the 16th hole — his fifth on the back nine — took him to −10.

Now atop the leaderboard, Player's par on 17 set the stage for one of the most extraordinary comebacks in

Gary Player celebrates after making a birdie on the 18th hole to seal his seven-shot comeback at the 1978 Masters.

Masters history. Player hit the fairway on the 18th hole and, with a 6-iron in hand, was ready to seal the deal.

"I put it in the middle of the green," he said, "and my caddie says, 'If you hole this, we'll win.'"

In his blue collared shirt and white pants, Player drained the 15-foot putt to cap off an incredible run of birdies that ultimately won the tournament. He had birdied seven of his final 10 holes to win his third Masters, after starting the day seven shots off the lead.

It was a near-impossible comeback. He shot a stellar 64 in the final round, including 30 on the back nine.

It had been four years since Player had won a major. But that day it didn't matter how far back he started. He knew all that matters is how things finish.

"Golf is not a game of 'ifs' and 'ands,'" Player said. "People talk about, 'This person did that, he did that.' The only thing that matters is what you score at the end. There are no remarks columns."

1978 MASTERS TOURNAMENT
FINAL ROUND

										ROUND 1	ROUND 2	ROUND 3	ROUND 4	TOTAL
										72	72	69	64	**277**
HOLE	1	2	3	4	5	6	7	8	9	10 11	12 13	14 15	16 17 18	TOTAL
PAR	4	5	4	3	4	3	4	5	4	4 4	3 5	4 5	3 4 4	**72**
PLAYER	4	4	4	2	4	3	5	5	3	3 4	2 4	4 4	2 4 3	**64**

Raymond Floyd watches his drive on the 7th hole during the final round of the 1986 U.S. Open at Shinnecock Hills.

RAYMOND FLOYD

OLD GUYS RULE AGAIN

1986 U.S. OPEN

FINAL ROUND

Nine weeks after Jack Nicklaus won the 1986 Masters, the focus of the golf world shifted to the U.S. Open at historic Shinnecock Hills. Few assumed, however, that another 40-something would be the one to keep an eye on during the national championship. In 21 attempts at the U.S. Open, Raymond Floyd had finished top-10 only twice. Now 43, he knew this might be his last chance, but a final-round blowout at a tournament the week before left Floyd angry and unable to focus. Refusing to let him stew, Floyd's wife pushed his buttons, forcing him to reset. The result was another major victory for the old guys.

Raymond Floyd, his daughter, Christina, and his wife, Maria, pose together after Floyd's comeback win to claim the U.S. Open Championship.

Following the final round of the 1986 Westchester Classic, Raymond Floyd and his wife, Maria, packed the kids, the nanny and all their stuff into the car for the two-and-a-half-hour drive to Shinnecock Hills on Long Island to begin preparations for the U.S. Open. Floyd was still fuming after blowing his chances of winning at Westchester. Having been tied for the lead at the start of the day, his final-round 77 saw him plummet to 12th place. It was a quiet drive to begin, and Floyd assumed Maria would just leave well enough alone and let him simmer. Instead she broke the silence by asking, "So what happened today?"

Floyd tried to brush aside her question, but Maria was persistent. "We have the U.S. Open this week, and I just want to know why this one got away."

"We golfers are pretty good at feeling sorry for ourselves, and the truth is I didn't have any good answers to her questions," Floyd said. "We rode along in an uneasy silence for a while, but Maria was unrelenting, demanding, 'Why don't you play well in the U.S. Open?' I was hot now, so I pulled the car over in the breakdown lane and we went at it. We screamed at each other, the kids were crying, it was awful. But it got me to thinking a lot. The end result was that we turned a negative into a positive."

1986 U.S. OPEN FINAL ROUND										ROUND 1		ROUND 2		ROUND 3		ROUND 4		TOTAL
										75		68		70		66		**279**
HOLE	1	2	3	4	5	6	7	8	9	10	11	12	13	14	15	16	17	18	TOTAL
PAR	4	3	4	4	5	4	3	4	4	4	3	4	4	4	4	5	3	4	**70**
FLOYD	4	3	4	3	5	4	3	4	4	4	2	4	3	4	4	4	3	4	**66**

He also realized his mental preparation for the U.S. Open had historically been hijacked by his feelings about the United States Golf Association setups. "[They] made these great courses something less than what they are meant to be — fairways choked too narrow and ankle-deep rough everywhere. I realized those bad setups led me to a bad attitude, which resulted in bad play."

Coming into Shinnecock for the tournament, however, his attitudes were challenged. The course had not been used for a U.S. Open for 90 years. Floyd had no previous experience to rate the USGA setup against. When he finished his practice round, he was delighted by the setup. "You could see it all; there was no trickery. The course didn't favor any type of player. You could play fades, draws, irons, whatever you wanted off the tee."

Floyd's tee time for the first round was just after 8 a.m. It was cold and rainy, and the winds were blowing 40 mph, at least. He shot a 75, but it could've easily been an 85 if not for his short game.

"I feel like that was the round that won me the U.S. Open," Floyd said.

"It was about survival."

Rounds of 68 and 70 had Floyd at +3, three shots behind the leader, Greg Norman. Sunday's round would have the makings of a bar fight.

"With nine holes to play, there were 10 guys within one stroke of the lead," Floyd said. "I think six or seven of them were already major champions. It was a power-packed group. But the one thing I knew about the final nine holes of a U.S. Open is that everybody starts making bogeys."

Chip Beck wasn't one of them. The newest student of teaching professional L.B. Floyd, Raymond's father, was on a tear. He made four birdies coming home but missed a 3-footer for another at the last to post a course-record 65. Lanny Wadkins, ever the gritty competitor, also posted a 65 but would need to wait it out. Hal Sutton, Ben Crenshaw, Mark McCumber and Bob Tway were all consumed by fate and circumstance in the struggle to get home.

Walking off the 10th tee, Floyd saw Maria in the crowd.

"She told me I had 'that look,' and once she saw that starry look 'like a racehorse with blinders on,' she knew

I had it under control," Floyd said. "She said she'd seen me win without that look, but she'd never seen me lose with it. She was right. Every shot I hit on the back nine, I felt like I had already hit it. It was a foregone conclusion. It felt wonderful."

When Floyd birdied the 11th hole he was in a nine-way tie for the lead, but he felt in control. A 20-foot par save at the next hole seemed to ignite a near-flawless sprint home, as Floyd hit every fairway and every green but one from there.

Floyd's fearless putter was also on display. He converted a birdie putt at the 13th hole, parred the 14th to grasp sole possession of the lead and then added another birdie at 16. After parring the final two holes, his final-round 66 was enough to pull out the win.

At 43 years and 284 days old, Floyd finally had his U.S. Open victory, becoming the oldest to win the national championship at the time. (A 45-year-old Hale Irwin would eclipse the mark four years later.) It was Floyd's fourth and final major.

"I knew it was a young man's game," Floyd said. "But as Maria told me, the ball doesn't know how old you are."

Jack Nicklaus watches as his birdie putt on the 17th hole in the final round of the 1986 Masters is about to drop. He birdied seven of the final nine holes to win.

JACK NICKLAUS

ONE FOR THE AGES

1986 MASTERS TOURNAMENT

FINAL ROUND

By the time Jack Nicklaus arrived at Augusta in 1986, he had lost his focus. He hadn't won a tournament in two years and hadn't won a major in six. He'd played so poorly leading up to the tournament that a good friend and golf writer made him a 100-to-1 longshot. But Nicklaus defied those odds and hung around the leaderboard into the fourth round. Then with four holes left to play, he turned back the clock and brought his entire focus back to the golf course for another shot at glory.

Bernhard Langer puts the green jacket on Jack Nicklaus following the Golden Bear's comeback for the ages.

"I really wasn't working at it that hard," Jack Nicklaus said of his golf game in 1986. "Did I try to prepare? Sure. But I didn't prepare to the extent that I did when I was right in the middle. I just didn't have any motivation to move in that direction."

Nicklaus was now 46 years old with an active family and several business ventures on the go, including a course design business. He was, in his own words, "an old guy out there playing golf who wasn't supposed to compete anymore."

With his focus elsewhere, Nicklaus went to Augusta and started through the motions. Little had been going right for him that spring except for one part of his game. He was putting very well after stumbling on a large-faced putter. The press immediately dubbed it the "omelet pan," and it was destined to become famous by Sunday night.

Nicklaus shot 74 in the opening round and was six shots behind the leaders. "I played pretty well, but I didn't make any putts," Nicklaus said. "I didn't putt very well."

But Nicklaus found reason for optimism. His ball-striking had been pure, so if he could find his putting touch again, there would be hope for the final three rounds.

Sure enough Nicklaus went out Friday and shot a 71, then followed that with a 69 on Saturday. He still wasn't anyone's choice to win a sixth green jacket, not with Seve Ballesteros, Greg Norman, Nick Faldo, Tom Kite, Tom Watson and Bernhard Langer all looking like potential champions. But Nicklaus had climbed all the way to eighth — just four shots out of the lead — and was starting to get a little buzz behind him.

On Sunday morning he received a call from his son Steve. In the course of conversation, Steve asked, "What do you think it will take, Pops?"

"I think 65 will win the tournament," Nicklaus replied. "I think 66 will put me in a playoff."

"Exact number I had in mind," his son told him. "Just go shoot it."

Through the first eight holes, however, Nicklaus hadn't done much to that end. He had a bogey and a birdie and was even par for the day. Then on the 9th hole, as he was preparing to putt a 12-footer for birdie, he heard a big roar coming from the 8th hole. Almost immediately he heard another from the same area, then another as several players all hit magnificent shots. Nicklaus turned to his playing partner, Sandy Lyle, and with a grin said, "Hey, why don't we see if we can make a little noise ourselves?" He then poured in the putt — the first of several as he set out on his famous march to another green jacket.

Nicklaus birdied the next two holes, bogeyed the 12th and then birdied again on the par-5 13th. He had hit four birdies in five holes and went on to par the 14th.

1986 MASTERS TOURNAMENT **FINAL ROUND**										ROUND 1		ROUND 2		ROUND 3		ROUND 4		TOTAL
										74		71		69		65		**279**
HOLE	1	2	3	4	5	6	7	8	9	10	11	12	13	14	15	16	17	18	TOTAL
PAR	4	5	4	3	4	3	4	5	4	4	4	3	5	4	5	3	4	4	**72**
NICKLAUS	4	4	4	4	4	3	4	5	3	3	3	4	4	4	3	2	3	4	**65**

On the par-5 15th hole, Nicklaus hit a perfect drive onto the fairway. With his son Jack Jr. his caddie that day, Nicklaus turned to him and said, "How far do you think a 3 will go here?"

Nicklaus meant a 3 on the score-card, and Jackie knew exactly what his father meant.

"He said, 'I think it will go a long way, Pops,'" Nicklaus recalled. "So I just took dead aim on it and it never left the pin. And then it started to trickle down to the left about 12 feet."

Nicklaus' adrenaline was riding so high that he had covered the 240-yard distance with a 4-iron. He strode up to the ball, bent over in his famous crouching stance and stroked it into the cup for an eagle.

Nicklaus had glanced at the leader-board before the 4-iron and saw Kite, Norman, Ballesteros and Watson all battling furiously to squeeze out an advantage. At last Nicklaus knew he was right in the heart of contention.

"Now I'm pumped," he said. "I know I'm just a couple of shots behind at that point."

At the 16th hole Nicklaus swung a 5-iron from 175 yards and heard his son say, "Be right," to which Nicklaus replied, "It is." The ball landed 12 feet from the hole, and Nicklaus made the putt. Augusta went crazy.

"It's kind of fun to go to a place and have it be wild again," Nicklaus said. "It had kind of been a few years since I'd seen any of that."

A drive and a wedge from 110 yards put him just 12 feet from the flag at the 17th hole for yet another birdie. Nicklaus now had sole possession of the lead. Up ahead was the final hole.

A perfect drive left him 175 yards to the flag. Unfortunately, just as he swung his 5-iron a gust of wind hit him in the face. He knew it wouldn't be good news. The ball dropped 40 feet below the pin.

But here Nicklaus had another secret weapon. His architectural company had redone the green during the summer of 1985, so he had intimate knowledge of it. He knew the putt would be faster than it once was but wouldn't have the extreme break of years past. With these thoughts in mind, Nicklaus stroked a perfect lag putt. One more tap-in and he had completed the back nine in 30 strokes for a final-round 65 — just as he'd predicted to Steve.

Nicklaus had done all he could. Now there was the matter of a 45-minute wait while Norman and Kite each tried to catch him.

The best push came from Norman, who had made four consecutive birdies and was tied for the lead heading into the 18th hole. Norman set up and hit his approach on the final hole from the middle of the fairway but blocked it into the crowd. He could only make bogey.

At 46 years old, Nicklaus was once again Masters champion.

It was quite possibly his most-watched win ever, with television cameras joining the live crowd that was trumpeting his every move for over two hours. Even today Nicklaus admits he gets tingles when he watches the old film of the Miracle of '86.

"It was just the end of a great week," he said. "It was not only fun, but it was something really neat to think that, you know, here I've come back. And I hadn't worked out. I'd been playing 12 tournaments a year, going through the motions."

Of all his victories, never did Nicklaus win as meaningful a title as the 1986 Masters.

Larry Mize jumps for joy after chipping in to win the 1987 Masters in a playoff.

LARRY MIZE

HOME SWEET HOME

1987 MASTERS TOURNAMENT

FINAL ROUND & PLAYOFF

Majors are remembered for many things. Who the protagonists were, where they fought and how they secured everlasting glory are all parts of the story. At times they are defined by prolonged battles and at others by a single astonishing, climactic event. A stunning and unexpected conclusion is exactly what Larry Mize authored at the 1987 Masters. That he did it at home with a sand wedge named for the player he grew up watching as a kid made it even sweeter.

Larry Mize hits a wedge at the 1987 Masters. His victory came after sinking a wedge shot in a playoff.

middle of it, you don't see it as you do from the outside."

Mize managed only par on the next two holes, so he knew he had to do something on the 18th. He had wanted to hit driver — had even taken it out of the bag — but he had also just watched Curtis Strange hit a 3-wood perfectly out by the bunker, leaving about 140 yards to the green. With a light breeze at his back, Mize turned to his caddie, Scott Steele, and said, "I think we should hit 3-wood too." Steele agreed, and Mize proceeded to hit his tee shot right beside the bunker.

Mize was pumped and settled on a hard 9-iron to get him the rest of the way. The pin was front-left and the greens were hard, but Mize hit a good shot at the pin. It landed, bounced up the hill and then bounced back down again to about 5 or 6 feet from the hole. Needing to make the putt, Mize was plenty nervous but was able to steady himself and knock it down.

That set up a three-way playoff with Ballesteros and Norman, two of the best in the world. But Mize wouldn't let himself get caught up in the star power surrounding him. He was a competitor, and he had a lot of experience.

"I'd played with both Seve and Greg and got along well with both of them

L arry Mize is a son of Augusta National and the only Masters champion to have come from Augusta. Growing up in the town known famously to host the Masters left a lasting impression on the four-time PGA Tour winner.

"As a boy my father took me to the Masters," Mize recalled. "I used to love to go to the range and just watch Jack Nicklaus hit golf shots, hoping to learn something from him."

In 1987 it was Mize who became the focus of attention as he worked his way into contention at Augusta National. There he took on two of the all-time greatest in Greg Norman and Seve Ballesteros for the right to slip on the green jacket.

"I cannot tell you I came into the 1987 Masters thinking I was going to

win," Mize said. "I had confidence and I believed I could win, but I kept my expectations in check . . . When I went to bed on that Saturday night I had a really good feeling. I'm not saying I knew I was going to win, but I had a really good feeling about the next day."

Mize's final round was hardly one for the ages. Through 15 holes, he yo-yoed between good and bad results. He did have five birdies, but every one of them was offset by a bogey.

Luckily for Mize no one else had been able to make a move. After bogeying the 15th hole, he looked at the scoreboard and saw that he was only one shot back.

"I said to myself, 'Okay, let's birdie the last three holes,'" Mize recalled. "Really this round was like a heavy-weight bout. When you're in the

1987 MASTERS TOURNAMENT
FINAL ROUND

										ROUND 1		ROUND 2		ROUND 3		ROUND 4		TOTAL
										70		72		72		71		**285**
HOLE	1	2	3	4	5	6	7	8	9	10	11	12	13	14	15	16	17	18	TOTAL
PAR	4	5	4	3	4	3	4	5	4	4	4	3	5	4	5	3	4	4	**72**
MIZE	4	4	5	4	4	2	3	5	4	5	4	2	4	5	6	3	4	3	**71**

PLAYOFF

HOLE	10	11	TO PAR
PAR	4	4	
MIZE	4	3	**−1**
NORMAN	4	4	**E**
BALLESTEROS	5	X	**X**

and had the upmost respect for them," Mize said. "But it was the birdie on the 18th hole that had me excited and confident about the playoff. My mind-set was do or die because there's no guarantee there will be another hole."

The playoff began on the 10th hole. Mize had been striking the ball well all week, and for once he was able to out-drive both Ballesteros and Norman.

"Normally, they're both 20 yards in front of me," Mize said. "But I was 20 yards in front of them . . . So when we hit our second shots, Seve hit it just off the green to the right, Norman hit just long, and I hit it about 10 feet under the pin. Perfect."

Both Ballesteros and Norman two-putted, Norman for par and Ballesteros for bogey, which would see him eliminated. That left Mize with a great chance to win it right there, but he missed the putt, letting a good opportunity slip by.

At the 11th hole things were back to normal as Norman's tee shot went 20 yards in front of Mize's. Norman was hitting an 8-iron to Mize's 5-iron. Mize tried to play a good shot, but his body got out ahead and the club behind him. He hit a flare out to the right about 100 feet from the hole.

"I was disgusted with myself," Mize said. "Scott, who was great all week and so calming, said, 'No biggie, we'll get it up and down.'"

Norman hit his 8-iron onto the right fringe, 40 to 50 feet away from the hole. That gave Mize a little hope for his next shot. If he could get it close, it might put some pressure on Norman.

For Mize, there was only one shot to play, and he knew exactly what he had to do. The shot called for a pitch and run. He figured it would have to land short of the green, because anything on the green would be too far and roll into the water. He also knew he had to use a sand wedge because anything with less loft would be too hot. The shot was out to the right and he had to be aggressive. "The pond wasn't really [a factor] in my mind," Mize recalled. "It was do or die."

Mize squared up his ideal shot and hit his spot. He then froze as he watched it roll.

"When it went into the hole I exploded and ran around screaming like a madman," Mize said. "Finally, I told myself, 'Settle down, you're screaming! Go get the ball and shut up!' I was just so excited. I couldn't believe it went in. It was total elation for me. It was incredible."

When Norman's putt for birdie slid past the hole, it was official. Mize's magical sand wedge had made history and secured his first and only major championship.

"The wedge I used that day was a Jack Nicklaus Muirfield 56° sand wedge," Mize said. "It was kind of funny. I used his wedge and then Jack put the green jacket on me. It was brand new that week. Augusta National requested a club that was instrumental in my win, so I gave them the sand wedge and it's now on display there."

A monument to a moment that will never be forgotten.

NANCY LOPEZ

OWNING THE LPGA CHAMPIONSHIP

⚑

1989 LPGA CHAMPIONSHIP

FINAL ROUND

Nancy Lopez is one of the best female golfers ever. A child golf prodigy, she won the New Mexico Amateur when she was 12 years old in 1969, then the U.S. Girls' Junior Championship when she was 15 and again at 17. While still an amateur, she was runner-up at the 1975 U.S. Women's Open. When she turned pro in 1977, her success continued. During her 20-year LPGA Tour career, she won 48 tournaments and sits seventh on the all-time wins list. Of her three major wins, Lopez's final victory came in 1989 at the LPGA Championship. It was yet another product of her relentless positivity and unwavering self-belief.

In May 1989 Nancy Lopez, 32 years old and the winner of 39 tournaments — including two LPGA Championships — was still every bit as competitive as she was when she'd been a plucky amateur tearing up the ranks. Her desire to win and always play her best was a trait her father, Domingo, had infused in her from a young age. He'd been her coach since she was 8 and was a constant positive influence in her life.

"That's what my dad was all about," Lopez said. "He always had something positive to say about a negative, and I think my whole life has been like that . . . If my dad ever had a negative face, I never saw it."

That positivity and belief in herself traveled everywhere with Lopez, and she brought it with her when she arrived at the Jack Nicklaus Golf Center in Mason, Ohio. It was the 12th consecutive time the LPGA Championship had been held there, and it would be the last, as the Senior PGA Tour was set to replace the women's event at the venue.

After scores of 71, 69 and 68, Lopez was looking good at 8 under par, but she wasn't in the lead. At –10, Japan's Ayako Okamoto was two shots clear of Lopez heading into the final round.

Lopez made up some ground on the first nine holes to tie Okamoto at –10 as the two made the turn. But on the 10th hole Okamoto sunk a 10-footer for birdie while Lopez three-putted, missing a 5-footer to save par. With one sloppy hole, Lopez had handed Okamoto back her two-stroke lead.

"That got me mad," Lopez said. "But it was a good mad . . . I really concentrated after that. The momentum was really changing quickly."

At the 11th hole Lopez chipped in for birdie, and the pressure was back on Okamoto. With laser focus, Lopez drained a 20-foot birdie putt at the 12th hole. A bogey by Okamoto on the same hole left Lopez feeling like she was in charge. Her mental strength had always set her apart from the pack. So with Okamoto reeling, she went for the jugular. Lopez birdied three more times on the final six holes.

"Ayako was still fighting, but at 17 I kind of knocked the breath out of her," Lopez said of her birdie on the second last hole. "On 18, that was such a thrill, such excitement. I could really feel the crowd pulling for me." Lopez birdied that hole as well, to close with an incredible 66.

"I concentrated so hard on every shot that when I looked at my scorecard and saw a 66, I was surprised."

Lopez defeated Okamoto by three

Nancy Lopez gets a hug from her daughter Ashley Marie in 1985. Lopez says family is as important as any golf championship is to her.

strokes and finished 14 under. Okamoto called her "number one."

It was the third, and final, major championship for Lopez — though she couldn't know that then.

For all that Lopez brought to women's golf, however, she still looks back on her career and life and feels like her three majors aren't even close to her greatest accomplishment.

"It was a fun career," Lopez said. "I was very blessed, but I have three wonderful daughters . . . I'd rather have my children because winning trophies is great but having a family is fantastic."

1989 LPGA CHAMPIONSHIP
FINAL ROUND

ROUND 1	ROUND 2	ROUND 3	ROUND 4	TOTAL
71	69	68	66	**274**

NICK PRICE

AN UNFORGETTABLE EAGLE

1994 OPEN

FINAL ROUND

As far as Zimbabwe goes, the list of internationally known athletes is short. In Duncan Fletcher, Heath Streak and Andy Flower, the country has some famous cricketers, while Bruce Grobbelaar was a big deal in soccer. In tennis there's Wayne Black, who collected over 18 doubles titles. Yet none compare to Nick Price and his three majors, especially the 1994 Open. There Zimbabwe's finest had to be clutch under pressure in Scotland. Price's trademark ball-striking was on full display as he edged Jesper Parnevik down the stretch, thanks to a stunning eagle.

Nick Price is arguably the most decorated Zimbabwean athlete of all time. He amassed 48 professional victories, including 18 on the PGA Tour. A former world number one, Price also won three major championships: the 1992 PGA Championship, the 1994 PGA Championship and the 1994 Open.

Of the three, Price's final round at The Open on the famed Turnberry golf resort in Scotland is one that will go down in golf lore.

Heading into Sunday, there was a sizable group of players in contention. As is always the case at major championships, the back nine was where things got interesting. Jesper Parnevik, who was playing in the group in front of Price, birdied the 11th, 12th and 13th holes to move to 11 under par and take the lead.

"Any time I get asked about The Open I refer back to the 16th, because I was two [strokes] behind Jesper playing 16, and I really had to have at least a birdie finish and hope he would drop a shot," Price said. "I was behind and odds were he was going to win."

Price — one of the Tour's best ball-strikers — put the ball in the fairway to give himself a chance. The hole was cut very close to the front, so Price played deep with his approach. He drew the ball off a bank to about 12 to 13 feet from the hole.

It was a tough downhill left-to-right putt, but Price poured it in. It wasn't the moment that history remembers, but it's the one Price does.

"Had I not made that," Price said, "it would have been very difficult for me to have won."

As Price walked to the 17th tee box, a par-5, he still found himself two back of Parnevik, as the leader had birdied 17 to move to –12.

Price, as per usual, hit a good tee shot and left himself a 5-iron to finish. He recalls that the green was difficult. "There were these little moguls in the front right-hand portion of the green, and anything short and right you'd have a tough chip or putt . . . so I wanted to hit past the flag and deep. I felt that was the percentage play."

With that goal he made his play. "I hit this beautiful cutting 5-iron in there, which pitched just left of the green."

But Price's shot ran up about 50 feet behind the hole, leaving him with a very long putt for eagle and what would be a share of the lead heading to the final hole.

"I just hit a really good putt," he said. "And as it went down the slope it went right over the spot that I had

Nick Price watches his birdie putt on the 4th hole during the final round of the 1994 Open.

aimed on and I thought, 'Well, this is going to be close.'"

About a foot and half before the hole, the ball hit a spike mark and bobbled. Fortunately for Price, it dived in the right-hand side of the hole.

Price couldn't contain his emotions. He pumped his arms, hugged his caddie and waved to the crowd emphatically.

Parnevik had bogeyed 18, and suddenly Price was walking to the 18th tee now one stroke ahead after being two behind. All he needed to do was control his golf swing for one

more hole and he would become an Open champion. Unsurprisingly he was pretty amped up on that final tee box, and he hit 3-iron for 275 yards — about 75 yards farther than normal. After a 7-iron and two putts for par, he had won his second major. An incredible –3 on the last three holes and a final-round 66 were enough to best Parnevik by one stroke.

"The relief of winning that was just huge for me," Price said. "I certainly favor that one victory in The Open Championship."

1994 OPEN FINAL ROUND										ROUND 1	ROUND 2		ROUND 3		ROUND 4				TOTAL
										69	66		67		66				**268**
HOLE	1	2	3	4	5	6	7	8	9	10	11	12	13	14	15	16	17	18	TOTAL
PAR	4	4	4	3	4	3	5	4	4	4	3	4	4	4	3	4	5	4	**70**
PRICE	4	5	4	2	5	3	4	4	4	4	3	3	4	4	3	3	3	4	**66**

DAVID DUVAL

DUVAL'S MAGIC NUMBER

⚑

1999 BOB HOPE CHRYSLER CLASSIC

FINAL ROUND

In 1999 David Duval became the third man ever to shoot a 59 in an official PGA Tour event, after Al Geiberger in 1977 and Chip Beck in 1991. What made Duval's 59 distinctive, unlike the first two, is that it came in the final round of the then 90-hole Bob Hope Chrysler Classic. Anyone who shoots a 59 knows they're joining an exclusive club. But in Duval's case the 59 had greater significance. He entered the final round seven back of the lead, and by the 18th hole anything less than an eagle wouldn't do.

David Duval was noted for being a stoic competitor in his day. If not devoid of emotion altogether, he was absolutely reticent to reveal any. So it was that his final round of 59 at the 1999 Bob Hope Chrysler Classic wasn't inspired by some heart-wrenching story, nor was it the result of some kindly twist of fate. Rather it was simply a manifestation of his golfing persona — a workmanlike, highly proficient execution of golf at its highest level.

It certainly wasn't looking that way before the tournament began, however. Anyone who watched Duval's pretournament practice session wouldn't have come away thinking this might be his day.

"I was a bit lethargic and just didn't feel like I had a ton of energy that morning," Duval said. But he perked up a little come the par-4 1st hole with a routine par that was a statement to himself.

"The most important shot of the day was that putt on the 1st green," Duval said. "I was struggling with my putter. I really was. I hit a beautiful wedge to 5 feet and I holed it. I felt I really needed to make that just for me, just to make a putt *now*. That was the most important part of the day."

Duval stroked a pair of 3-foot putts for birdie on each of the next two holes. Then after parring the 4th he made birdie again on the 5th to put him 4 under par after just five holes. He stayed there as he parred the next three holes, but at the 9th, he was back in business with another birdie. Halfway through his final round Duval was 5 under par.

Duval's recounting of the beginning of his back nine is as methodical as was his play:

"At the par-4 10th I hit 3-wood, then sand wedge to 4 feet for birdie," Duval said. "The [par-5] 11th was driver, then I hit a 4-iron kind of long and left, then had a pitching wedge to 4 inches for birdie. At the par-3 12th I hit a 6-iron to 2 feet for another birdie."

Those three holes and three birdies had him at –8 for the round.

Duval parred the 13th hole from 12 feet. Then on the par-5 14th he found trouble off the tee after hitting his driver into the bunker. But Duval was able to get a 5-iron on it and left himself a wedge in. He hit it to 10 feet and made the putt for birdie.

At the par-3 15th hole Duval hit an 8-iron to 1.5 feet and made the putt. His 2-iron then sand wedge at the par-4 16th got him even closer for birdie. After a 6-inch tap-in, Duval was now 11 under par for Sunday's efforts.

After only parring the 17th hole,

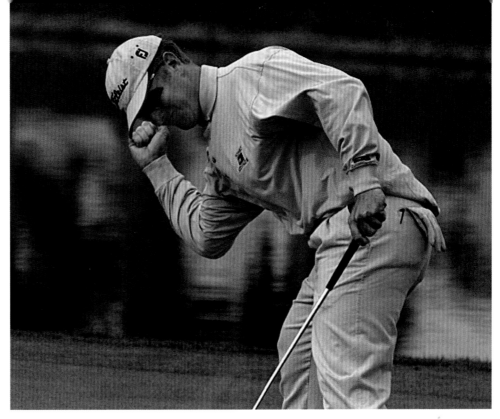

David Duval celebrates his eagle on the 18th hole during the final round of the Bob Hope Chrysler Classic. The 2-under-par stroke tied him for the then-lowest round in PGA Tour history.

however, Duval would need to execute some heroics on the final hole to go sub-60 and get the win.

With the adrenaline pumping on the 543-yard par-5 18th, Duval drove his tee shot much farther than he expected. It left him just 218 yards to the hole. A 5-iron got him to the green in two, giving him a shot at the eagle he needed to make history and win the tournament.

"I am not going to say that you stop trying to think about it because you can't," Duval said of his chance for eagle. "I took a couple of deep breaths and just hit it and thought I'd see what would happen."

What happened was a significant slice of history. With his 8-foot eagle putt, Duval became just the third man to shoot a sub-60 round. He needed every bit of that 59 to catch the leader, Steve Pate, who shot a more than respectable round of 66 himself. In the end Duval won by a single stroke.

"It is something you don't think about," Duval said. "It is just not something I expected to do in my career, certainly not in tournament golf."

1999 BOB HOPE CHRYSLER CLASSIC **FINAL ROUND**								ROUND 1		ROUND 2		ROUND 3		ROUND 4		ROUND 5		TOTAL
								70		71		64		70		59		**334**
HOLE	1	2	3	4	5	6	7	8	9	10	11	12	13	14	15	16	17	18	TOTAL
PAR	4	5	3	4	3	5	4	4	4	4	5	3	4	5	3	4	3	5	**72**
DUVAL	3	4	2	4	2	5	4	4	3	3	4	2	4	4	2	3	3	3	**59**

Paul Azinger follows his shot from the seventh tee of the Waialae Country Club during first round play of the Sony Open in Honolulu.

PAUL AZINGER
TRAGEDY TO TRIUMPH

2000 SONY OPEN

FINAL ROUND

Paul Azinger: a name synonymous with grit and glory. In 1993, he ascended to the sport's zenith, a major champion, an eleven-time PGA Tour victor and a stalwart of Team USA. His fierce rivalry with Seve Ballesteros was legendary, but it was outdueling Nick Faldo that brought him the most satisfaction. While Azinger's career spanned an era marked by legends like Watson, Nicklaus and Woods, it was his tenacity that distinguished him from his competition. However, beneath the triumphs, he fought a silent battle with cancer that threatened to extinguish his brilliance. Despite the doubts that followed, Azinger's remarkable return to the winner's circle was a beacon of hope and inspiration.

Paul Azinger kisses his golden trophy after winning the Sony Open at the Waialae Country Club in Honolulu.

W hen Paul Azinger won the 1993 PGA Championship, he seemed to be at the height of his power. By then, he was a major champion, an eleven-time winner on tour and a dependable, steely-eyed member of Team USA who would not back down to anyone — least of all Seve Ballesteros, a fierce competitor who seemed to have everyone else's number.

"I always wanted to be Seve," Paul admits. "I wanted to be the artist, the creative genius he was. Everyone saw us as ardent competitors, and we were, but we grew to have great respect for each other. Now, who did I have the most fun beating in my era? That'd be Nick Faldo. He was the engineer,

someone who wanted to win the most, and I got the most satisfaction from beating him."

Azinger was authoring his impressive career resume at the same time as Seve, Nick Faldo, Nick Price, Fred Couples and Payne Stewart, and while legends such as Tom Watson and Ray Floyd were still highly competitive. Azinger's career bridged the time of Jack Nicklaus, right up to the era of Tiger Woods' dominance.

"I loved the time in which I played. I would not trade it for anything. To have been able to compete and win against the giants of my time is something that I'm proud of."

But while Azinger had felt that satisfaction plenty of times, during

the focus and ultimate euphoria of his major championship, he felt something else.

"In '93 my right shoulder was really hurting me. I just figured it was just one of those things, you know, we all had something hurting at one time or another. But Dr. Frank Jobe wanted to biopsy my shoulder and I didn't want to, so in June he did a bone scan, and he didn't like what he saw. Dr. Jobe actually called me on the Friday night of that PGA Championship and said he wanted to do a biopsy that following Tuesday, so I knew there was something serious going on — a problem. I asked him to wait until after the following month's Ryder Cup. That really kind of added to my sense of urgency at the PGA. I thought it was going to be rotator cuff surgery or something like that and it would sideline me for a season, which seemed like an eternity. I was blindsided by the fact that it was cancer. It changed everything. It changed my life, it cut my playing career short, no question about it. But life is funny, and I was given the gift of being able to perform that week despite my lingering worry, to win that PGA, play in another Ryder Cup and Presidents Cup. And without that PGA victory, I would never have been the 2008 Ryder Cup captain."

2000 SONY OPEN FINAL ROUND										ROUND 1		ROUND 2		ROUND 3		ROUND 4		TOTAL
										63		65		68		65		**261**
HOLE	1	2	3	4	5	6	7	8	9	10	11	12	13	14	15	16	17	18	TOTAL
PAR	4	4	4	3	4	4	3	4	5	4	3	4	4	4	4	4	3	5	**70**
AZINGER	4	4	4	3	4	4	3	3	5	3	3	4	3	4	4	4	2	4	**65**

Retrospect and gratitude heal a multitude of wounds, but the intense treatment for lymphoma, and the lengthy recovery of his strength, touch and confidence would prove to be mentally, as well as physically, taxing. Sometimes his doubts were the loudest voices.

"You don't ever try to imagine what would have happened without getting sick. As you get older, you start to think more about it. I was a pretty confident player. I might not have been number one, but in my brain I was. I had a ridiculous run. But after the cancer, especially in the first three or four years after, the thought of winning again on tour was just not something I believed possible. I was never going to win on tour again, I had no doubt about that. I was playing that bad. I just didn't see it coming back."

However, seven years after his PGA Championship victory, the now 40-year-old Azinger has rediscovered his touch, thanks to a new long putter anchored into his abdomen and a new perspective gained from losing two business associates and his best friend, Payne Stewart, in a jet crash.

"It was a very sad off-season. That tragedy changed my whole focus."

Azinger entered the final round of the 2000 Sony Open after rounds of 63, 65 and 68. He pulled away from the field that Sunday with a bogey-free 65 that added up to a seven-shot victory over Stuart Appleby.

"I felt terrific. I had some anxiety when I got there. I didn't know what to expect. But I was determined not to get ahead of myself."

Still, Azinger's amazing return to the victory circle after cancer, seven years of competitive purgatory and the tragic loss of his friends all seemed to be a beacon of sorts.

"The inspiration was there, but the whole divine intervention thing was a little too much to ask at that time. It was up to me and I did what I had to do."

Understandably, this win felt different than all the others. After everything, this was not just about celebrating; this win seemed to tie together so much more.

"That day I thought about people who have dealt with cancer and are dealing with it now. I was lucky to get a lot of support that really encouraged me. But most people don't get that. I wanted to be the source of encouragement for them. Life has so much heartaches. Life has some sad moments. I didn't know that until I experienced them. The [jet crash] accident at the end of the year changed the way I perceived life. It was difficult to feel the same joy like when I won the PGA Championship. That unencumbered joy, seeing life through rose-colored glasses. I didn't wear those glasses anymore."

Sometimes, hardship can bring a change in perspective, motivation and purpose.

"I believe that everything about life is purposeful. We were created with a purpose, and my belief: I think back on the increments of my life and everything is purposeful in each phase of life, as a player when my family and I were younger, and now that I cannot compete anymore, now I talk for a living. As I get older, I have a more charitable mindset, I want to be of service to others more. We all hit a fork in the road at some point at each phase of life. I'm not who I was, but I'm happy with who I am. I've had an exciting life."

FIRST TIME'S
THE
SWEETEST

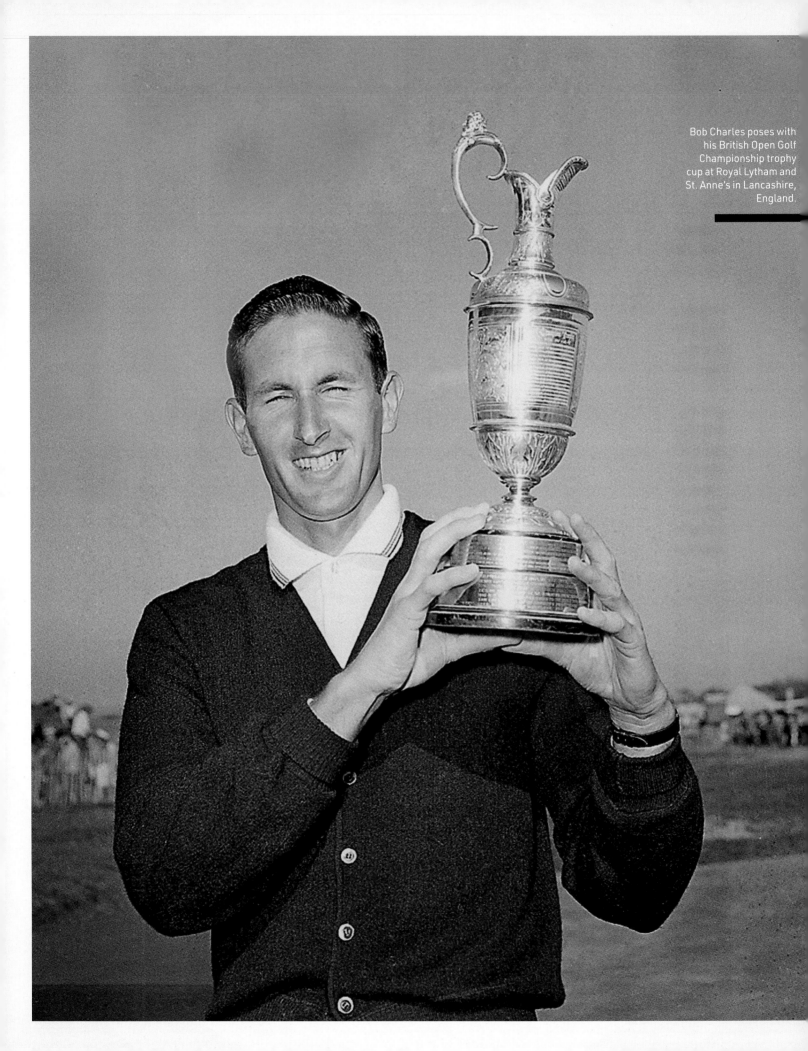

Bob Charles poses with his British Open Golf Championship trophy cup at Royal Lytham and St. Anne's in Lancashire, England.

BOB CHARLES
THE FIRST

1963 OPEN

FINAL ROUND

In the rich tapestry of golf history, there stands a unique figure: Bob Charles of New Zealand. He achieved an extraordinary feat: he clinched a win at the 1963 Open at Royal Lytham & St Annes and became the first left-handed golfer to win a major championship.

Bob Charles sends out a plume of sand as he hits out of a bunker at the third hole against Phil Rodgers in the British Open Championship Playoff at the Royal Lytham and St. Anne's Club in Lancashire, England.

G olf has been around for centuries, so can you imagine being the first to do something in a major championship victory? What's more, can you imagine being the last? For New Zealand's Bob Charles, being the first time was nothing new. "When I turned pro, nobody in New Zealand had ever become a touring professional."

Bob Charles won the 1963 Open at Royal Lytham & St Annes and was also the first lefty to ever win a major. He accomplished the same feat of distinction as the first lefty to win on the PGA Tour in April of that year, when he won the Houston Classic, bolstering his confidence further.

"When I went to London in July of '63, I felt there were probably only five players that I had to beat," recalls Charles, "and that was [Arnold]

Palmer, [Gary] Player and [Jack] Nicklaus and the other two were the two Australians Kell Nagel and Peter Thomson. At that stage, Tony Jacklin hadn't come on the scene, while I think he did play in the event, he wasn't one of the recognized better players in the UK at that time. So, all I had to do was beat those five and there I was."

Charles had a mindset that placed him in the company of Palmer, Player and Nicklaus — then known as the "Big Three." Palmer's most prolific years were from 1960 to 1963 when he won 29 times on the PGA Tour, including five major championships in four seasons. Palmer is often credited with re-opening the gates to The Open in the minds of American professionals who for the most part had competed sparingly in The Open

post–World War II. The irrepressible Player was established as a three-time major champion and the 23-year-old Nicklaus was already a two-time major winner. Nicklaus had taken down Palmer the year prior at the U.S. Open at Oakmont and added his second major at Augusta National early that year.

"My career was overshadowed by the Big Three, Arnold Palmer, Gary Player and Jack Nicklaus, but I did take great pleasure on the odd occasions when I beat them."

Such was the case at the 1963 Open.

"Nicklaus bogeyed the last two holes to miss out on the playoff with me and Phil Rodgers by one stroke," explained Charles. "But he went on to win the PGA Championship the very next week in Dallas, Texas. In my day, the longest hitter out there was Jack Nicklaus, 275 yards on the average, I was 25 yards behind him. My strength was my fitness and my putter."

Charles had an ingrained love for The Open that stretched back to his days playing with his father.

1963 OPEN
FINAL ROUND

ROUND 1	ROUND 2	ROUND 3	ROUND 4	TOTAL
68	72	66	71	**277**

"My father used to always say as he faced a putt he had to be make, 'This one is for The Open.'"

Charles' father introduced him to golf, but his inspiration came from within. "In 1954, I started a subscription to Golf World. Golf World together with a book by Henry Cotton gave me an insight into the world of golf outside of home in New Zealand. Ben Hogan's book Power Golf became a part of my library, and I spent many an hour standing in front of a mirror trying to replicate that near perfect swing."

One might wonder if standing in front of a mirror for "many an hour" was the root of his left-handed swing — one of the most memorable images of his victory at The Open — but Charles says it came naturally.

"Nobody can get their head around this, but I'm right-handed — I write with my right hand, I play tennis with my right hand. But whenever I grip anything with two hands, it's instinctive for me to put the left hand below the right and stand on the right-hand side of the ball, hit it on the right-hand side of the club and hit it to my right. For example, if I pick up a rifle, I put the left hand below the right hand. If I pick up a pool cue, I put the left hand below the right hand. A spade, an axe, everything I do with two hands, I put the left below the right. And swing obviously … with an axe I swing it over my left shoulder."

Charles intimated that this righty-playing-lefty approach might be a key to his putting prowess at The Open.

"I don't consider myself a left-handed golfer. I'm a back-hander. I prefer to use backhand, I play a double-handed backhand. I stand on the right side of the ball, I hit the ball on the right side of the clubface and I'm hitting to my right. Now when I'm lining up a putt, I'm looking at the hole and the ball with my strong right eye. So, I've got a feeling … well, it's not a feeling. I've got a theory, I suppose, is the best way of describing it. If you're left-eyed, you should be a right-handed putter; if you're right-eyed, you should be a left-handed putter. I think you get a better perception, better depth perception. If I'm looking to my right, to my strong side, visually I get a better picture looking right than looking left. My strong right eye is looking at the target,

the hole, to my right rather than to my left.

"It was on the putting green, over the putter, that won the tournament for me as is the case for most people when they win golf tournaments. You can't win golf tournaments without being a good putter. I had a great week, the putter was red-hot and to have to go through a 36-hole playoff on that Saturday, was an endurance contest."

The 36-hole playoff that Saturday was Charles' other point of disctinction, having triumphantly achieved something that will never happen again.

"1963 was the last time they used a 36-hole playoff, as the format changed to 18 holes the following year. We played 18 holes on Wednesday and Thursday, 36 on Friday and the 36-hole playoff on Saturday. 72 holes in two days and 108 holes in four days to secure the Claret Jug."

Charles' recipe for success that day was two-fold: his putting prowess and his fitness over 36 grueling holes.

"When I got to the 36-hole playoff on the Saturday, I thought I had a good chance of winning. Dare I say it, but Phil Rodgers was a slightly overweight fella and I thought my fitness would have worked in my favor and so it proved. In the playoff I won pretty comfortably."

The lean-and-lanky Charles had beaten the young American by eight shots in the playoff, acknowledging his play had "demoralized" his opponent through his flat belly and flat stick.

"It was my putter that won this championship."

KEN VENTURI

A MAJOR TO DIE FOR

⚑

1964 U.S. OPEN

FINAL ROUND

Shortly before the U.S. Open in 1964, Ken Venturi was ready to walk away from the game and go sell cars instead. It had been four years since he had won on the PGA Tour, and he hadn't even been invited to play in that year's Masters. But after an invitation to Westchester, Venturi finished third at the tournament and took home a decent check, ending his career as a car salesman before it even began. A couple weeks later he would get an even bigger check, when he risked death trying to win the U.S. Open.

I n 1964 the U.S. Open was held in mid-June at the Congressional Country Club in Maryland, just outside the nation's capital. The event was still contested as a 36-hole final on Saturday, and the week had been exceptionally hot. Temperatures were hovering at or above 100°F (38°C), pushed considerably higher by the heat index. As if the heat wasn't enough, 33-year-old Ken Venturi was already starting to suffer from the nerve damage in his wrists that would ultimately close out his competitive days a couple years down the road.

"I haven't told many people, but on that Friday night, I went to a local church and asked the priest to pray with me," Venturi said. "I was asking God for the strength to believe in myself."

Venturi would need all the help he could get.

"There was a draw for caddies in those days, and I had drawn William Ward. Pure luck. He was Congressional's best caddie. Maybe fate was looking out for me."

With his lucky draw, Venturi worked steadily but still found himself six off the lead held by Tommy Jacobs. The course was the longest in U.S. Open history up until that point, which, despite Venturi's penchant for being one of the longer hitters on Tour, was compounding issues.

Ken Venturi makes his final putt of the 1964 U.S. Open. Venturi overcame severe dehydration to win the tournament.

"I didn't think I had much of a chance to make up that much ground, to be honest," Venturi said. "But you never know. 'It's the U.S. Open,' I told myself."

On Saturday morning everything began to click for Venturi. His opening-nine score was an astonishing 30. He finished the round with a 4-under-par 66, bringing him to within two shots of Jacobs. His score would've been even better, but Venturi tired as the round drew to a close. He bogeyed the 17th and 18th holes from distances of just 18 and 30 inches.

By now the heat was really getting to Venturi. In between rounds he tried as best as he could to get ready for the afternoon. But he wasn't feeling well and was on the verge of fainting. That's

when Congressional member Dr. John Everett found him lying on the floor in front of his locker. Everett told Venturi he was suffering from dehydration and should call it quits because continuing to play might prove fatal. But Venturi refused. Instead he took some drastic measures to get ready for the final round.

"The doctor told me if I went out and tried to play, it could be fatal. I told him it was better than the way I'd been living. So I took 18 salt tablets," Venturi said, "[and] we now know that many can also kill you."

On the 1st tee it was so hot that Venturi lay down for a few minutes to rest. He doesn't recall any of his shots on the front nine, except his putt at the 9th hole.

"I had doctors, marshals, a cop, a whole entourage following me, so the gallery knew what was going on," Venturi said. "When that putt dropped I was leading the U.S. Open. When it fell, the sound was deafening and it helped me."

Throughout his final round, Venturi faced some difficult bunker shots. But he wouldn't play it safe. His last bunker shot came on the 18th hole. After he made it, he had only about 10 feet for the win.

"When that putt dropped," Venturi said, "I raised my arms and said to myself, 'My God, I've won the Open.'"

Venturi had shot a final-round 70 to win by four shots. He'd managed to hold it together through the heat of the summer and the pressure that comes with a U.S. Open. But when 21-year-old Raymond Floyd came up to congratulate him, Venturi finally let it all out.

"I had control over my emotions up until then," Venturi said. "But Ray bent down and picked my ball up out of the hole for me. When the young man handed me the ball, he had tears streaming down his face." That's when Venturi broke down.

"I just lost it."

1964 U.S. OPEN **FINAL ROUND**										ROUND 1	ROUND 2	ROUND 3	ROUND 4	TOTAL
										72	70	66	70	**278**
HOLE	1	2	3	4	5	6	7	8	9	10 11 12 13 14 15 16 17 18				TOTAL
PAR	4	3	4	4	4	4	3	4	5	4 4 3 4 4 5 3 4 4				**70**
VENTURI	4	3	4	4	4	5	3	4	4	4 4 3 3 5 5 3 4 4				**70**

KATHY WHITWORTH

SIMPLY THE BEST

⚑

1965 TITLEHOLDERS CHAMPIONSHIP

FINAL ROUND

The best golfer in history is a subjective topic. But in golf, winning is synonymous with greatness — you simply cannot have one without the other. So with that in mind, if someone asked who the all-time winningest golfer in history is, one might say Sam Snead, Ben Hogan, Arnold Palmer, Gary Player, Jack Nicklaus or Tiger Woods. But any of those answers would be wrong. The answer is Kathy Whitworth. Her accomplishments are both legion and legendary. The World Golf Hall of Fame member won a staggering 88 times on the LPGA Tour and finished runner-up 95 times. Her titles include six major championships, the first of which Whitworth won in record-breaking fashion.

Although still in its infancy, the LPGA Tour was entering its 16th season in 1965, with 30 official money events scheduled between March and November. There were established stars in the sport as well. Mickey Wright had already won more than 60 tournaments, and Betsy Rawls had more than 40 wins. Kathy Whitworth, who had turned pro in 1958, was well on her way with 11 victories of her own, and she was just learning how to win.

"Winning is just who has the lowest score — just focus on your own game, do the best you can and [do] not worry about who is around you," Whitworth said. "I hardly ever even knew who I was playing with. That is a discipline you have to learn."

As the season wore on, Whitworth found her stride, winning seven tournaments from March through October. By the time the season-ending 1965 Titleholders Championship arrived, she had 18 wins. She had yet to win a major, but she felt her game was ready for the pressure of playing in major championships, where every shot counts.

"One shot at a time is just so crucial," Whitworth said. "That is the only shot you have any control over . . . It's not being afraid to lose, it's trying to win."

The Titleholders Championship was the LPGA Tour's version of the Masters. It had always been contested in April at the Augusta Country Club in Georgia; this was the first year it was played in November.

After rounds of 71, 71 and 74, Whitworth had put herself in a great position to win her first major. At even par she had a five-shot lead. Heading into the final round, she decided she wouldn't hold anything back.

"Why go out there if you weren't trying to win, because that was the motivation," Whitworth said. "I can't think of any other reason to go out there and practice and work."

Whitworth got off to a bit of a rocky start with three bad holes early in her round. But the mental strength she had built within herself would pay dividends.

"You have to learn to concentrate, and you have to learn to control your emotions," she said. "There were times when I did get pretty nervous . . . It's all up to you and how you deal with it."

Whitworth not only dealt with it, she shattered the tournament record for the widest margin of victory. Three early bogeys were balanced by finishing her round with three birdies to close out the tournament at −1, a full 10 shots clear of second place. Her cumulative winning score of 287 was the lowest ever in the tournament by two shots. Whitworth's astounding margin of victory to collect her first major and

Patty Berg puts the green champion jacket on Kathy Whitworth after she won the 1965 Titleholders Championship.

her eighth win that season was enough to earn her that year's Associated Press Female Athlete of the Year award.

If you're looking for a lesson in how to win at life, look no further than Whitworth.

"I do tell young players when I can . . . just do the best you can," Whitworth said. "If you want to dig a ditch, just be sure it's the best ditch ever."

Sound advice for golf and life from the winningest golfer in history.

1965 TITLEHOLDERS CHAMPIONSHIP
FINAL ROUND

ROUND 1	ROUND 2	ROUND 3	ROUND 4	TOTAL
71	71	74	71	**287**

HALE IRWIN

SOLE SURVIVOR

⚑

1974 U.S. OPEN

FINAL ROUND

*In 1974 the United States Golf Association designed a monster
18 holes that slayed many of the game's greatest. Gary Player, Jack
Nicklaus, Johnny Miller, Arnold Palmer, Billy Casper and Tom
Watson all succumbed to the cruel course. Yet Hale Irwin remained
optimistic and even had a dream that he would tame the wild beast
and win his first U.S. Open. He told no one but his wife about his
ambition before setting to work on living his dream.*

Hale Irwin gestures to the gallery in the mid-1980s.

I t's called the Massacre at Winged Foot, as legendary journalist Dick Schaap coined it. Not exactly the most endearing of names. The 1974 U.S. Open held at Winged Foot Golf Club's West Course in Mamaroneck was, by many accounts, the most difficult U.S. Open setup of all time.

Gary Player called it the "toughest test of golf I'd ever seen." Tom Watson described the course as "a monster." Even Lee Trevino weighed in, saying, "You had to be lucky or a magician to get the ball anywhere near the hole, just for par."

Such was the backdrop for a major that will never be forgotten for its severity and the impact it had on the game's biggest stars.

Hale Irwin, however, came into the tournament full of confidence, knowing a win would be a dream come true. He brought with him an extra dose of conviction that this would be his major championship breakthrough.

"A couple of weeks before the U.S. Open I told my wife I had a dream I'd won the tournament," he said. "I never told anyone other than her. I haven't told anyone else because I knew how they would react. It happened. I told my wife and I've not told anyone else because I didn't think people would believe me."

The thing that was truly unbelievable, however, was how hard Winged Foot was to play.

Even before a single golfer posted a score in the tournament, there were grumbles. "It's a mental battle," Irwin said of playing the setup. "By the time my practice rounds were done, 70 percent of the field was just gone. You could hear it in the locker room

and dining area. The players that didn't have the confidence or where-withal to fight that battle were already done. I had to maintain a realistic attitude about what I could accomplish and have a plan going in about what I could do, not what I couldn't do. That's too negative."

The prevailing thought as to the toughness of the setup goes back to Johnny Miller's final-round 63 at Oakmont the year before. Some have said it prompted the USGA to ensure no such heroics could be employed at Winged Foot. However, Sandy Tatum, a member of the USGA executive committee in charge of the course, was emphatic there was no connection between Miller's score and the difficult setup at Winged Foot.

"The media approached me after the first round as though we had done something wrong, asking if we were trying to embarrass the best players in the world," Tatum recalled. "'No' I replied. 'We're trying to identify them.'"

The stars were out in full force at Winged Foot. Player won the Masters that April, Nicklaus was an ever-present threat, Trevino was at the height of his prowess, Miller was the defending champion and Arnold Palmer was showing good form. There was also a host of other established

1974 U.S. OPEN FINAL ROUND										ROUND 1	ROUND 2	ROUND 3	ROUND 4	TOTAL
										73	70	71	73	**287**
HOLE	1	2	3	4	5	6	7	8	9	10 11 12 13 14 15 16 17 18				TOTAL
PAR	4	4	3	4	5	4	3	4	4	3 4 5 3 4 4 4 4 4				**70**
IRWIN	4	4	3	5	5	4	3	5	3	4 3 5 4 3 5 5 4 4				**73**

and up-and-coming players all looking for more. Among them were major champions Tony Jacklin and Billy Casper, as well as those who would inherit the game, like Watson.

"I was aware of the players around me — great players," Irwin said. "But I only concentrated on me and what I could afford."

For Irwin, that meant getting a good start on every hole.

"Driving the ball was so critically important," he said. "Once you hit the fairway, though, you had to get it on the greens under the hole. I tried to do that all week. I'd rather I had a 30-foot uphill putt than a 10-foot downhill putt. You had to have a plan. You could not attack most of the holes. On that course you had to take what you could get."

At the end of the first round, Player led with a level-par effort of 70, with Irwin tied for ninth at 3 over. The field average was almost 78 that day.

In the second round Irwin's 70 jolted him up the leaderboard, tying him with legends Palmer and Player and another major champion in Raymond Floyd. In the third round Watson shot the round of the day,

posting a 69 to move to 3 over par and take sole possession of the lead. Irwin shot 71 and stood one shot back of Watson heading into Sunday. Third place belonged to the 44-year-old Palmer, who was only three strokes off the lead on a course where three shots could be found on one hole.

The final round carried with it all the drama of a U.S. Open and all the angst this particular one forged in abundance. Watson and Irwin battled as best as they could in the opening holes until Irwin finally broke free.

"I birdied the 9th hole to take sole possession of the lead," Irwin said. "It was a switch in momentum on that hole. I felt like it was my tournament to go out and win. It was the mind-set I needed to get myself into."

Irwin bogeyed the 13th hole before bouncing back with a birdie on the 14th. When he reached the final two holes, Irwin was forced to make a critical putt on the 17th after two bad shots.

"I thought, 'I've got to make this,' because in those days you really didn't know where you stood because they didn't have leaderboards everywhere like they do today," Irwin said. "It had

at least a foot to a foot and a half of break. I made the putt and thought, 'What a big, big putt!' On the way to the 18th tee a marshal told me I had a two-shot lead, so that putt gave me the confidence to play 18 as well as I did."

On the final hole Irwin's tenacity in brutal conditions was once again on display when his nearly worn-out 2-iron produced another majestic shot to set up the win. After two-putting the 18th green, Irwin secured his first U.S. Open title. In a field stronger than any before it, his winning score of +7 was the second highest since World War II.

"Of all the U.S. Opens I've played," Irwin said, "Winged Foot in '74 was the most difficult . . . In my playing years there's no doubt it was the most difficult golf course I've ever played."

Irwin went on to win two more U.S. Opens, in 1979 and 1990. Whether this particular victory was the catalyst or a confirmation of greatness to come, Irwin's place among the immortals in the World Golf Hall of Fame attests to his accomplishments.

"For me," Irwin said, "winning the 1974 U.S. Open was literally a dream come true."

BERNHARD LANGER

ONE FOR ALL OF GERMANY

1985 MASTERS TOURNAMENT

FINAL ROUND

Everyone expected one of the game's big names to come away with the green jacket at the 1985 Masters, and through three rounds it looked like one of them would. But a late fourth-round charge from a relative unknown upset everyone's expectations. For Bernhard Langer it was the difference between a solid career of modest fame and a life of sporting immortality as a major champion — Germany's first ever.

When Bernhard Langer was a kid growing up in postwar Germany, his homeland wasn't exactly known for churning out golfers. The sport wasn't a priority, at any level, and hardly any opportunities existed for a young boy aspiring to be a golf professional.

Langer, however, was lucky.

"Germany was in a rebuilding process, and there were very, very few golf courses — less than 100 in the whole country," Langer recalled. "I was fortunate enough to grow up five miles from one of those golf courses."

Because of that proximity to the club in Augsburg, Langer caught the golf bug at the age of 9 when he started caddying alongside his brother.

"I just fell in love, at first with earning money; then I immediately fell in love with the game."

As a teenager Langer tried his luck in the amateur ranks in his home country until a lower back injury in training for his mandatory military service nearly ended his career. But he recovered, and in 1975 he got his first professional win, at the German National Open Championship. It was an event he would win 12 times in his Hall of Fame career.

By 1976 Langer had earned his way onto the European Tour, and in 1980 he won his first event, the Dunlop Masters.

At that time the golfers on the PGA Tour and European Tour rarely played events on each other's circuits, and the Ryder Cup had yet to become the massive event it is now. So Langer was still a bit of an unknown in the United States, even though he had played the Masters twice and also had two near misses on the world stage at The Open, finishing second in both 1981 and '84.

There were no world rankings in existence yet, but everyone knew who the big guns were as the 1985 Masters got under way. Curtis Strange, Raymond Floyd, Tom Watson, Lee Trevino, Gary Player and Seve Ballesteros were all expected to be in the mix for the green jacket.

Through the first two rounds Langer was quiet. Scores of 72 and 74 left him six shots back of the lead. His third-round 68 threw him into contention, but halfway through the final round he sat well back of Strange, who birdied four of his first eight holes to jump out to a four-stroke lead. For his part Langer kept his focus only on what he could control.

"I was trying to make a conscious effort to not watch the leaderboard that day," he said.

Langer then went on a run for the

1984 Masters champion Ben Crenshaw pats 1985 Masters champion Bernhard Langer on the back after Langer became the first German to win a major.

ages. His birdie putt on the 12th hole grabbed the right edge of the cup and circled a full 360 degrees before diving into the hole. On the next hole, his 195-yard approach on the par 5 led to an easy two-putt birdie.

"I could sense that I was close, but I didn't know exactly where I was," he said. "I could tell I was definitely in the hunt."

After Strange bogeyed the 13th and 15th holes, finding the water on both, Langer took control. A great approach shot on 15 set him up for an easy two-putt birdie, and another flawless approach two holes later set up his

fourth birdie in his previous six holes.

"When I birdied 17 I looked at the leaderboard and I saw that I had a two-shot lead," Langer said. "It gave me a sense of, well, it's not over yet . . . but I figured a par or bogey would be good enough."

Indeed it was. Langer bogeyed the 18th hole to finish 6 under par — two shots clear of Strange, Ballesteros and Floyd.

Langer had done it. He'd become the first German to win one of golf's four major championships. It was the first of two Masters titles for Langer, who would win his second in 1993.

"It was a dream come true," he said.

1985 MASTERS TOURNAMENT **FINAL ROUND**										ROUND 1		ROUND 2		ROUND 3		ROUND 4		TOTAL
										72		74		68		68		**282**
HOLE	1	2	3	4	5	6	7	8	9	10	11	12	13	14	15	16	17	18	TOTAL
PAR	4	5	4	3	4	3	4	5	4	4	4	3	5	4	5	3	4	4	**72**
LANGER	4	6	3	3	3	3	4	5	4	4	4	2	4	4	4	3	3	5	**68**

TOM LEHMAN

A CAREER-DEFINING VICTORY

1996 OPEN

FINAL ROUND

1996 was a transitional year in PGA history. The Tour was still dominated by those we now refer to as legends, players like Tom Watson, Greg Norman and Fred Couples. But young stars like Phil Mickelson (four wins) and Tiger Woods (two wins) were beginning to cement their status. However, for Tom Lehman, the three-time All-American from the University of Minnesota, it was his best year: he was named PGA Player of the Year and PGA Tour Player of the Year; he won the Vardon Trophy and the Byron Nelson Award, and he was the Tour's leading money winner. More important, however, Lehman captured his lone victory at a major — and it was all thanks to his suddenly magic putter.

 eading up to the 1996 Open, Tom Lehman had yet to win on tour that year. But he was on a tear, having already collected 10 top-10 finishes, including a runner-up effort at the Buick Classic as well as at the U.S. Open just a couple weeks prior to the event.

"Going into that British Open I was definitely playing well, you know," Lehman said. "And I knew I was capable of winning a major."

The 125th edition of The Open was held at Royal Lytham & St Annes Golf Club in England. After three rounds Lehman had put himself in position to win his first major. With a third-round 64, he held a six-shot lead at 15 under par.

Entering the final round, Lehman knew this event was his to lose. As he made the turn, he was holding things together nicely. He'd dropped only one shot, at the par-4 3rd hole. All week long his putting had been the difference.

"The putter was magic," he said. "When the putter got working that way I could really separate myself from the field because I generally hit the ball well . . . Whenever I really putted well I had the chance to win and win by a lot."

There are turning points in every round, and the 12th hole was one for Lehman. By his own admission, he hadn't been playing his best. But he was hanging in there, and on 12 he had a chance to turn it around.

"It's the hardest par 3 on the course," Lehman said. "I hit a great 4-iron and made a beautiful putt . . . I felt so much better after that."

Lehman's major was within reach after his par save out of the left bunker on the 15th hole. That put him three shots up with only three holes left. He told himself to just keep it simple.

"Play the game, play the hole, play the shot," he said.

Lehman played the final three holes 1 over par to shoot a final-round 73, two shots clear of Ernie Els and Mark McCumber. He'd done it. Lehman was the 1996 Open champion.

"It was kind of a validation for all the hard work and proved finally once and for all that I was capable of winning a tournament like that," Lehman said. "To me the pinnacle was to win a major and to become world number one."

As Lehman's only major championship, it is his career-defining victory

Tom Lehman kisses the Claret Jug after winning the 1996 Open at Royal Lytham & St Annes Golf Club.

— and the culmination of a player's pure love for the game.

"You cannot be your very best unless you love it," Lehman said. "If you don't love it, you're not going to work hard enough and commit enough and sacrifice enough. Love for the game is really the foundation for anything you are doing . . . If you don't love it and you aren't passionate about it, you will never ever achieve true success and be as good as you could be."

That day at the 1996 Open brought the best out in Tom Lehman.

1996 OPEN
FINAL ROUND

	ROUND 1	ROUND 2	ROUND 3	ROUND 4	TOTAL
	67	67	64	73	**271**

HOLE	1	2	3	4	5	6	7	8	9	10	11	12	13	14	15	16	17	18	TOTAL
PAR	3	4	4	4	3	5	5	4	3	4	5	3	4	4	4	4	4	4	**71**
LEHMAN	3	4	5	4	3	5	5	4	3	4	5	2	4	5	4	4	5	4	**73**

Padraig Harrington plays an uphill shot on the 3rd hole during the final round of the 2007 Open at Carnoustie.

PADRAIG HARRINGTON

PADRAIG'S BELIEF

2007 OPEN

FINAL ROUND & PLAYOFF

*By the time he made it into the clubhouse after his final round,
Padraig Harrington thought he had given away the 2007 Open.
His double-bogey on 18 conjured images of Jean Van de Velde's
triple-bogey at the 72nd hole in 1999. That effectively handed the win
to Scotland's own Paul Lawrie, and in 2007 Harrington thought he
had done the same for Sergio Garcia. But after being gifted a second
chance, Harrington wasn't about to let his first major victory get away
again. He sealed the deal in a four-hole playoff over Garcia to become
the first Irishman in 60 years to win The Open.*

Padraig Harrington chips the ball across the Barry Burn after taking a drop for playing into the water during the final round of the 2007 Open.

I n 2007 the 136th Open returned to the formidable Angus links named Carnoustie. Owing in part to Ben Hogan's 1953 victory there, the one and only time he competed in the event, the course has always carried with it an air of being unyielding. Contributing to its reputation is the list of other legendary champions who have prevailed there, including Tommy Armour, Henry Cotton, Gary Player and Tom Watson.

Such was the collective mind-set heading into the 2007 Open. No one was quite sure what to expect, except perhaps Padraig Harrington.

"I said to those with me that week I was going to win The Open," he said. "It's not that I had a vision or something. It's like I was trying to plant the concept in my mind so it wasn't so distant a possibility. I felt totally comfortable with where I was that week — my game and my mind."

To the rest of the world, the prospect of the 35-year-old Harrington breaking

through and winning his first major wasn't so assured. He started the final round six shots behind Sergio Garcia, who seemed to be cruising along comfortably since opening with a 65; Harrington was to play in the second to last grouping and Garcia the last.

Both men started strong as they each birdied the 3rd hole. Harrington was feeling confident.

"[It] was the first major I felt totally comfortable and focused," Harrington said. "[I] stayed focused on me, not everyone else. I cannot control what they do."

Harrington certainly couldn't control what Andres Romero was doing. Playing a few groupings ahead, the young Argentinian posted 10 birdies on the day and at one point held the lead, but a double-bogey at the 17th undid the charge. Garcia, on the other hand, played drastically different golf than he had in the three previous rounds. He made a bogey at the 5th and another at the 7th, and he followed that up with yet another on the 8th. After

the back-to-back bogeys, he gathered himself to par the next four holes — but the door had been opened.

Harrington, meanwhile, birdied the 9th hole to pull within one shot of Garcia and then made a strong par-saving putt on the 10th. He caught Garcia with a birdie on the 11th.

With Garcia making birdie on 13 to once again lead by one stroke, self-belief and a commitment to the game plan proved critical for Harrington on the par-5 14th.

"Nothing had happened in the round up until that point that caused me to think, 'This is my day,'" Harrington said. "I had a number of putts that sat on the lip, a number of putts that were ever so close. Normally, when it's your day, you chip in or hole a long putt. None of that was happening until I got a very good break at 14."

Going for the green in two, Harrington assumed his ball had kicked just left of the green. He thought it was going to be about 30 feet from the hole. Instead he was just 15 feet away. He had gotten the big break he was looking for, and he sealed it with an eagle.

If Harrington was looking for omens, however, his final hole in regulation wasn't the one he wanted. Garcia bogeyed the 15th, which meant

FINAL ROUND

	ROUND 1	ROUND 2	ROUND 3	ROUND 4	TOTAL
	69	73	68	67	**277**

HOLE	1	2	3	4	5	6	7	8	9	10	11	12	13	14	15	16	17	18	TOTAL
PAR	4	4	4	4	4	5	4	3	4	4	4	4	3	5	4	3	4	4	**71**
HARRINGTON	4	4	3	4	4	4	4	3	3	4	3	4	3	3	4	3	4	6	**67**

PLAYOFF

HOLE	1	16	17	18	TO PAR
PAR	4	3	4	4	
HARRINGTON	3	3	4	5	**E**
GARCIA	5	3	4	4	**+1**

Harrington held a one-shot lead on the tee box as he played the last hole.

The 18th at Carnoustie is famous for the Barry Burn — the narrow, rock-faced river that winds itself through the course. On 18 it is devilishly situated at the end of the fairway, about 30 yards short of a green protected by bunkers on either side at the front and by out-of-bounds areas to the rear. The legendary water hazard has ruined many rounds, none more spectacularly than Jean Van de Velde's bid for the 1999 Open. Needing only a double-bogey to walk away as champ, Van de Velde tripled the hole and lost his best shot at a major in a playoff.

For Harrington the Barry Burn caused similar heartache. He found the burn not once but twice. His drive, which nearly made it across the footbridge to safety, cruelly fell into the water, forcing a drop that he hit fat and that also took the plunge. Yet even after his two dreadful shots, Harrington was able to regroup on the green, such was his laser focus that week.

"There were moments walking up the fairway where I was thinking that I couldn't believe I had lost The Open this way," Harrington said. "I was embarrassed by the mess I had made and the people I had let down. But I had such strong belief in what we were doing that week that by the time I reached the green I was back in the zone."

Harrington dropped his putt to post a double-bogey and then had to wait for Garcia to finish. Garcia needed a par to win, but his putt curled off the left edge of the cup, giving him a 38 on the back nine. Garcia and Harrington were off to a four-hole playoff, starting at the 1st, then moving to 16, 17 and the treacherous 18th.

Harrington birdied the first playoff hole, while Garcia made bogey, and both posted pars on the next two holes to set up a thrilling 18th in which Garcia needed to find two strokes to stay alive.

Not wanting to find the burn again, Harrington played it safe and in doing so opened up an opportunity for Garcia, who had made a difficult shot from the rough to make the green in two. Harrington was on the green in three, and his long par putt was up first. He missed, leaving himself 3 feet for bogey. A birdie for Garcia would extend the playoff, but as it had been all Sunday, his putt narrowly missed the hole. Harrington calmly holed his bogey to win the Claret Jug.

When asked after the round about becoming the first Irishman to win The Open in 60 years, Harrington played up the enormity of the moment by admitting just how humbled he was by it all. "It's going to take a long time for it to sink in," he said.

Justin Rose poses
with Merion's signature
wicker flags and the
championship trophy
after winning the
2013 U.S. Open.

JUSTIN ROSE

MORE HISTORY AT MERION

⚑

2013 U.S. OPEN

FINAL ROUND

Justin Rose is too young to be inducted into the World Golf Hall of Fame, but there is little doubt he's headed there. He has 23 worldwide victories and counting, including nine on the PGA Tour and 12 on the European Tour. His biggest victory to this point remains the 2013 U.S. Open at the historic Merion Golf Club. On the same course that immortalized a legend back in 1950, Rose channeled his inner Ben Hogan to win his first major.

Justin Rose kisses the U.S. Open Championship Trophy after his two-stroke victory at Merion in 2013.

T he East Course at Merion Golf Club is in Haverford Township, Pennsylvania. The history there is significant. The club was founded all the way back in 1896, and its two golf courses opened in 1912 and 1914. The East Course was one of the first in the United States designed to incorporate penalties for straying offline as well as various options for players coming into the greens. It was so innovative, in fact, that in 1992 the club was designated a National Historic Landmark. Prior to the 2013 tournament, it had hosted four U.S. Opens, in 1934, 1950, 1971 and 1981.

The 1950 U.S. Open is of particular importance. The legendary Ben Hogan had been in a life-threatening car accident in 1949 and was told he would never walk again, let alone play golf. He miraculously recovered and went on to win the 1950 U.S. Open in

a playoff at Merion. In the final round, with his legs barely functioning, Hogan struck his now famous 1-iron from the 18th fairway. The shot was immortalized by photographer Hy Peskin in what many consider one of the greatest sports photos ever taken. To this day, there is a plaque commemorating the shot in that very spot on the fairway.

It was on that same fairway that the 2013 U.S. Open would be decided. But Merion Golf Club wouldn't give up great shots so easily that year.

For all that Merion has given to the game of golf, it also happens to be a difficult course. At the 2013 U.S. Open, the average score in each of the four rounds was 74, which was 4 over par. Justin Rose was able to navigate the challenge masterfully with scores of 71, 69 and 71 through the first three rounds.

"I had committed myself to the process that week," Rose said. "I committed

myself to putting a strategy in place."

Heading into the fourth round at 1 over par, Rose trailed Phil Mickelson by two shots for the lead. It also happened to be Father's Day, and the significance wasn't lost on Rose. He had lost his father to leukemia in 2002, and being a father himself, he had his kids' names stitched onto his shoes. To top it off, Rose's swing coach, Sean Foley, sent him a message before his final round.

"He sent me a text and told me to go out there and be the man my dad taught me to be and the man that would make my kids proud," Rose said. "So he kind of brought it to two generations for me. Being Father's Day, obviously it was sweet for me on both levels."

The final stretch to victory wouldn't be easy, however. The course played just as difficult on Sunday, and through 10 holes it was a three-man

2013 U.S. OPEN **FINAL ROUND**										ROUND 1	ROUND 2		ROUND 3		ROUND 4			TOTAL
										71	69		71		70			**281**
HOLE	1	2	3	4	5	6	7	8	9	10	11	12	13	14	15	16	17	18	**TOTAL**
PAR	4	5	3	5	4	4	4	4	3	4	4	4	3	4	4	4	3	4	**70**
ROSE	4	5	4	4	5	3	3	4	3	4	5	3	2	5	4	5	3	4	**70**

Justin Rose salutes the gallery after his par putt on the 18th hole during the final round of the 2013 U.S. Open.

race. Rose and Mickelson, who had eagled the 10th hole, were tied at even par, as was Jason Day, who had crawled into contention. Rose three-putted the 11th hole but came back with birdies on 12 and 13 to take the lead.

"I felt like I got my momentum back on the stretch of 14 to 18," Rose said. "I felt like it gave me a little bit of wiggle room coming down the stretch, which I think everybody needed on this golf course."

Rose headed to the final hole needing at least par. Just as Hogan had done in 1950, Rose got to the 18th fairway and relished the opportunity.

"The Hogan 1-iron," Rose said, "that's an image all of us have grown up seeing . . . That image is kind of hard to escape. This was my turn to kind of have that iconic moment."

With a 4-iron in hand and Hogan's 1-iron in mind, Rose found himself in the same spot Hogan had been in 1950. The significance wasn't lost on Rose at the time.

"I had plenty of time on the 18th to realize that this was my moment," he said. "I have seen that Ben Hogan photograph a million times, and suddenly it was me hitting from the middle of the fairway."

Standing near Hogan's hallowed ground, Rose deposited his ball just off the green. He had set himself up nicely for the par he needed.

The weight of history couldn't defeat Rose that day, as he became the first Englishman in over four decades to win the U.S. Open after Mickelson failed to make the birdie he needed on 18 to force a playoff. Rose finished 1 over par for the tournament, winning by two shots over Mickelson and Day.

Looking skyward after his victory, Rose knew he had accomplished something that would've made his dad proud and something that will always make his children proud of their dad. And he'd done it in Hogan-like fashion.

"It is a surreal moment when it actually happens," Rose said. "[It is like] you are living out of a dream at that point."

ADAM SCOTT

BREAKING THE CURSE

2013 MASTERS TOURNAMENT

PLAYOFF

For both Australia and Adam Scott, the 2013 Masters cast out many demons. No Australian had ever won a green jacket, and whispers had grown louder that Scott couldn't handle the crucible of major championships. Only the summer before he appeared poised to win The Open before bogeying the final four holes to let that major slip away. To most this was another indication of his unfulfilled potential. Yet to Scott it was confirmation that he was good enough to contend on the big stage, and he used that motivation at Augusta in 2013.

Australia has produced its fair share of world-class golfers. Peter Thomson, Greg Norman, David Graham, Jason Day, Steve Elkington, Kel Nagle, Jim Ferrier and Geoff Ogilvy are all major champions. What is shocking is that none of them ever won the Masters. It's not as if they hadn't tried. In fact, eight times Australians had finished second at the Masters — until Adam Scott came along in 2013.

"Australia is a proud sporting nation, and this was one notch in the belt that we never got," Scott said. "It's amazing that it was my destiny to be the first Aussie to win it."

Early in the 2013 Masters, however, destiny looked to have chosen two other Aussies. Through the first round, countryman Marc Leishman held a share of the lead with Spaniard Sergio Garcia after both shot 66. Then in the second round Day posted a 68 to take sole possession of the lead. Scott, however, was certainly in the mix, sitting three shots back after the second round.

Saturday saw Angel Cabrera and Brandt Snedeker ascend to the top of the leaderboard with rounds of 69. Scott also shot a 69 to put him one stroke off the lead heading into Sunday; both Leishman and Day were one shot behind him.

Contenders in the final round were greeted with cold temperatures and rain — weather that seemed to fore-shadow Scott's poor start on Sunday.

It began with a drive off the 1st tee going left. That forced Scott to punch a 6-iron from about 145 yards, bump and run a 7-iron and then two-putt for bogey. On the 2nd hole he hit a 3-wood into the right rough and had to lay up with a 6-iron. From there he hit a lob wedge to the fringe and two-putted for par.

"It wasn't the start I wanted," Scott said. "I felt like I gave two strokes back to the field."

Scott got back on track on the 3rd hole when he converted a 20-foot putt for birdie. He thought it might be the start of something, but he could only make par over the next nine holes. Luckily he was only two shots behind Cabrera for the lead.

Scott then made birdies on 13 and 15. By the time he reached the par-4 18th hole, he sensed a birdie might just be enough to win the Masters.

Adam Scott roars to the sky after making a birdie putt on the second playoff hole to win the 2013 Masters.

2013 MASTERS TOURNAMENT
PLAYOFF

HOLE	18	10	TO PAR
PAR	4	4	
SCOTT	4	3	-1
CABRERA	4	4	E

A driver and an 8-iron left him with a 25-foot putt.

"When I made the birdie putt, for a moment I thought I had won," Scott said. "I had gotten a bit defensive on the front nine and felt like I wasn't being bold enough. On that putt I just trusted."

Playing in the group behind Scott, Cabrera needed a birdie at the last to force a playoff. A brilliant approach to 3 feet ensured a birdie and the tie.

Both Scott and Cabrera made par at 18, the first hole in the playoff; the pair then moved on to the par-4 10th hole, where two good tee shots and approaches followed. Up first on the green was Cabrera, and his putt for birdie slid past the hole.

By then it was getting dark, and the pair wasn't going to play another hole that night. The Aussie curse looked like it would live another day. But Scott had other ideas.

"I was thinking, 'I don't want to have to come back tomorrow,' because I was thinking I wouldn't be sleeping," Scott said. "It was my first ever putt to win a major."

With an entire country behind him, Scott drained the putt left-center. The curse was broken. The two players embraced after Scott's first major championship.

"It was all such a blur, euphoric," Scott said. "[Cabrera] could not have been happier for me. The golf we played in the playoff was spectacular."

Sergio Garcia celebrates after making his birdie putt on the 18th green to win the Masters and finally capture his first major after 73 prior attempts.

SERGIO GARCIA

MASTERING THE POSITIVE

⚑

2017 MASTERS TOURNAMENT

FINAL ROUND

No one ever doubted Sergio Garcia's natural talents. But after 73 prior attempts at major championships, including 23 top-10s, 13 top-fives and four second-place finishes, he had no victories in golf's grandest events. Garcia knew he was "the best player never to win a major," and to change that unofficial title he had to block out such noise. At the 2017 Masters he did just that. Playing with the same unbridled emotion as always, Garcia came away with his first major and his first green jacket, with a little help from a Spanish legend.

Sergio Garcia basks in the moment after receiving his green jacket for winning the 2017 Masters.

T he Masters has a way of cutting through the wrinkles of time and bridging events decades apart. When Jose Maria Olazabal was about to play the final round of the 1994 Masters, he found a note of encouragement in his locker from another Spanish superstar, Seve Ballesteros. Olazabal won that day. A similar thing happened in 2017, when Olazabal told Garcia he wanted to share a locker with him in the Champions Locker Room at Augusta.

"It was very special because he's my idol," Garcia said. "He and Seve are both my golfing idols since I was very, very little."

Since turning pro in 1999, Garcia had won several times on the PGA Tour. But by 2017 he still had not won a major.

"Am I ever going to win one?" Garcia said of his thoughts. "I've had so many good chances, and either I lost them or someone has done something extraordinary to beat me. So [my never winning a major] did cross my mind."

But the 2017 Masters was different. It wasn't about what hadn't been, but what could be. It wasn't about measuring shortcomings or focusing on negativity. It was about embracing the positive. With good vibes flowing all around him, thanks to those closest to him, Garcia couldn't help but look on the bright side. As his lockermate Olazabal told him, "You know what you have to do. Just believe in yourself."

Along with the boost of confidence he received from Olazabal, Garcia had another source of positive vibes,

FINAL ROUND

	ROUND 1	ROUND 2	ROUND 3	ROUND 4	TOTAL
	71	69	70	69	**279**

HOLE	1	2	3	4	5	6	7	8	9	10	11	12	13	14	15	16	17	18	TOTAL
PAR	4	5	4	3	4	3	4	5	4	4	4	3	5	4	5	3	4	4	**72**
GARCIA	3	5	3	3	4	3	4	5	4	5	5	3	5	3	3	3	4	4	**69**

coming from his fiancée (now wife), Angela Akins. That week she flowered the couple's rented house with little yellow sticky notes of positive quotes and letters of encouragement from those closest to them, such as "Don't forget to be amazing!"

"A lot of great notes from family, friends, throughout the beginning of the week and a lot of cute and beautiful notes from my fiancée were stuck on the mirror of the bathroom," Garcia said. "All those things helped a lot."

But even with all the help, Garcia's major breakthrough wouldn't be easy.

Through the first three rounds, he was tied for the lead with Justin Rose at 6 under par. Rickie Fowler was one shot back, and Jordan Spieth was among a group two behind. This part of the script wasn't any different from countless of his other tries at a major.

Nor was it any different in the fourth round. Garcia birdied the 1st and 3rd holes to jump two shots clear of Rose. Soon his lead was extended to three after Rose bogeyed the 5th hole.

Garcia was steady, posting pars through the rest of the front nine. But almost on queue, Rose went on the attack, making three consecutive birdies on holes 6, 7 and 8 to tie Garcia as they made the turn.

The golf world likely sensed what was on the horizon. And Garcia delivered. Two disappointing drives into the pine straw on both the 10th and 11th holes led to bogeys for Garcia, handing Rose a two-shot lead. It was expected, unfortunately for Garcia, that Rose would go on to win as fate had preordained so many times before.

Both men parred the next two holes, but at the 14th hole Garcia got a shot back, thanks to his 9-iron approach to about 5 feet. His modified claw-grip putting grip resulted in a birdie that clawed him back within one of Rose. Then at the par-5 15th hole, Garcia made one of his best shots all week.

"I hit an 8-iron from 189 yards, a little bit down breeze and downhill," Garcia said. "It looked like it glanced the pin and finished 12 to 15 feet away, where I made a putt for eagle."

Garcia's eagle and Rose's birdie had the duo tied atop the leaderboard, three clear of the rest of the field.

At the 16th hole Rose made yet another birdie and now held sole possession of the lead at –10. But a bogey at the next dropped him back to –9, tied with Garcia through 71 holes.

At the 18th Garcia hit a great wedge from 133 yards uphill to set himself up for birdie and the win. But he missed the putt, and the two would need to go to a sudden-death playoff. The world had seen this situation play out painfully for Garcia at the 2007 Open. But this script would be different. Garcia wouldn't allow himself to wallow in self-pity, remembering that one of Angela's posted messages was "Nothing is impossible; the word itself says, I'm possible!"

Back at the par-4 18th for the first playoff hole, Rose found the trees with his drive and was forced to chip back to the fairway. Garcia's drive was in the fairway, and from 145 yards uphill he hit a 9-iron to about 12 feet. Rose was on the putting surface in three shots, facing a 14-foot putt for par. When he failed to convert it, Garcia had the luxury of two putts to win his first major championship. He needed only one. "Curled it in there nicely," he recalled.

And with that, a curse — and a long major winless drought — was over. Garcia was positively the 2017 Masters Champion.

Lilia Vu celebrates her playoff win against Angel Yin in the Chevron Championship women's golf tournament at The Club at Carlton Woods.

LILIA VU

A GRANDFATHER'S LESSON

2023 CHEVRON CHAMPIONSHIP

FINAL ROUND

In 2023, Lilia Vu clinched her first major championship at the 2023 Chevron Championship at Carlton Woods, echoing the sentiment that "everything happens for a reason." Her journey to victory was inspired by her grandfather, Dinh Du, whose bravery shaped their family's destiny. This win wasn't just about golf for Vu: it was a tribute to her grandfather's courage, reminding her to "try her best" in the face of adversity.

Lilia Vu reacts to her playoff win against Angel Yin in the Chevron Championship women's golf tournament at The Club at Carlton Woods.

"Everything happens for a reason," reflected Lilia Vu after securing her first major championship, the 2023 Chevron Championship at Carlton Woods. "I just try to stay positive and try not to be too hard on myself and have fun. We all know the end goal, what I want to do is win. Just not getting too far ahead of myself, letting the golf do its thing and trying my best."

"Trying my best" is a simple formula for success. But for Vu, it has become a mantra built on her grandfather's love and the extraordinary risk he took that changed the lives of a desperate community of people. Vu's grandfather and his incredible bravery and vision have become her model of how to perform on golf's grandest stages.

Seven years after the end of the Vietnam War, Vu's grandfather, Dinh Du, set his sights on leaving Vietnam with his family for a better life. Each night under the cover of darkness, Du would sneak into the jungle where he was secretly building a boat by hand. His plan was life threatening, but he hoped this would be their deliverance. One night he returned from the jungle and told his family that they need to depart immediately. Vu's mother,

2023 CHEVRON CHAMPIONSHIP FINAL ROUND										ROUND 1	ROUND 2		ROUND 3		ROUND 4		TOTAL
										68	69		73		68		**278**
HOLE	1	2	3	4	5	6	7	8	9	10	11	12	13	14	15	16	17	18	TOTAL
PAR	4	4	3	5	4	4	3	5	4	4	4	3	5	4	4	4	3	5	**72**
VU	4	3	2	5	4	4	3	4	5	4	4	3	5	4	4	4	2	4	**68**

Kieu Thuy, remembers she and her sister running through the jungle to the boat. As they set off, desperate members of their community jumped into the water and swam out to them. Although the boat was only made to accommodate 52 people, Du did not turn anyone away and they eventually left with 82 people aboard. After two days at sea, Du sent up an emergency flare as their overburdened craft began taking on water. The group was eventually rescued by a United States Navy warship.

Vu always remembers what her grandfather did to save their family and pave the way for her to pursue her dream.

"The last thing he told me was to play my best," Vu recalls. "Even today, I was getting really upset on the course. I just had to remind myself, like, Grandpa is with you, and he'd be really disappointed if you were getting upset like this and that you didn't get your act together."

Vu is a former number one ranked amateur and was a great golfer at UCLA, but that does not mean that Vu's path to a major championship

was easy. After a bumpy start as a rookie on the LPGA, Vu contemplated walking away from professional golf. That's what happens when you make one cut in nine attempts. And so, Vu was demoted to the Epson Tour. When her grandfather died at the start of the COVID pandemic, she was left searching for reasons to continue. Eventually, she found a path out of the jungle of her doubts by reading personal development and self-help books. Fast forward to 2023, and she is a multiple-time LPGA winner.

"Everything happens for a reason. All the bad things, everything I've ever struggled through, family-wise, internally. I think of myself as the biggest obstacle. I mean, I had a pretty tough, not easy, past two days. I was definitely my own enemy, and I don't know how I pulled this out."

Vu pulled out this major victory with impressive tenacity and grit. Entering the final round trailing leaders Angel Yin and Allisen Corpuz by four strokes, Vu started to make up ground on the front nine, where she posted a score of 2 under par. Her back nine was steady, highlighted by

birdies at the 17th and 18th holes to hold the clubhouse lead that eventually led to a playoff with Angel Yin. In the playoff, Yin found the water on her approach while Vu fired an adrenaline-fueled 7-iron into position that would eventually set up a 14-foot birdie putt to secure her victory.

"I can't even put into words what I was feeling. I was nervous. I was scared. I was cold. I just wanted to hit the putt and just be done with it. I just saw my line and speed — I knew it was going to be a fast putt — and trusted myself."

Vu can reflect on her journey through the prism of her grandfather's journey: "I was just in such a bad place with my golf game. Just everything was life or death. I just saw everybody that I've competed with being successful, and I just compared myself all the time. But now I know that everybody's journey is different."

Thanks to her grandfather, Vu knows that some journeys are literally life and death; a golf round is nothing to fear.

AN UNDERDOG'S TALE

JACK FLECK

THE MUNICIPAL PRO

1955 U.S. OPEN

FINAL ROUND

Few knew his name, much less anything about the man who was chasing down a living legend. Contrary to media reports, Jack Fleck wasn't a "driving range pro," but he did come from humble roots as the son of an Iowa farmer, and he served in the Navy during World War II. As such, not much could intimidate the man. So when Ben Hogan carried a seemingly insurmountable lead into the clubhouse, Fleck was undeterred. Patiently and methodically he chipped away at his idol's lead, and the roar from the crowd on 18 told Hogan that this major was far from over.

Jack Fleck watches his birdie putt on the 18th hole during the fourth round of the 1955 U.S. Open. His birdie tied Ben Hogan for the lead.

At the age of 43 Ben Hogan was still the purest ball-striker on the PGA Tour. But after a phenomenal 1953 season, in which he'd won three of the four majors, he'd gone winless the following year and was looking to end that streak at the U.S. Open in 1955.

As always his preparation was meticulous. Hogan arrived a week early to study and practice at the recently toughened up course. So too did an unknown golfer named Jack Fleck. The preparation paid dividends for both golfers.

After the first three rounds Hogan was in sole possession of the lead, followed by Sam Snead and Tommy Bolt, one and two strokes back, respectively. Meanwhile Jack Fleck, who was three shots back, had become the tournament's Cinderella story. His final round remains the stuff of fairy tales.

Perhaps more so than any other tournament, the U.S. Open seems to garner stories of the otherworldly. Fleck was an enigma, virtually unknown to fans and media. He had been prying away at professional golf but had little to show for it. Then in 1955 everything came together at Olympic, including his putting, which had never been one of his strengths.

"There was something about that week," Fleck said. "I was so calm. During the second round I felt an almost tingling feeling in my hands, and from that point on I felt like I couldn't miss with my putter."

The U.S. Open was still played as a 36-hole final in 1955, and this one would be remembered for the eventual 1-on-1 showdown between Fleck and Hogan.

Hogan teed off for his fourth round in the early afternoon ahead of a number of his pursuers, including Fleck. In an arduous final round, it appeared that Hogan had secured his fifth U.S. Open title when he posted an even-par 70. Gene Sarazen, who was doing television commentary, rushed up to Hogan as he walked off the 18th green and congratulated him on his victory.

Hogan said all the right things about there still being players on the course who could catch him, but Sarazen pressed, asking Hogan to hold up his hand, signifying "five," as in becoming the first to win five U.S. Opens. It wasn't like Hogan to be boastful, yet he seemed to do it before realizing its significance.

"It's not over yet, Gene," he said.

Once committed, however, the act instantly became golf's version of "Dewey Beats Truman," the infamous headline from the *Chicago Daily Tribune* in November 1948, incorrectly pronouncing the upstart Thomas Dewey as defeating incumbent president Harry Truman.

Fleck was on the 10th tee when Hogan finished his round, and through his first nine holes he had cut Hogan's lead down to one stroke. Fleck was fully aware he was chasing down a legend. "I was fortunate to do the playing at that time I did . . . There was no time at all that I felt scared or under pressure coming down to the wire."

1955 U.S. OPEN FINAL ROUND										ROUND 1	ROUND 2	ROUND 3	ROUND 4	TOTAL
										76	69	75	67	**287**
HOLE	1	2	3	4	5	6	7	8	9	10 11 12 13 14 15 16 17 18				TOTAL
PAR	5	4	3	4	4	4	4	3	4	4 4 4 3 4 3 5 4 4				**70**
FLECK	5	5	3	4	4	3	3	2	5	3 4 4 3 5 2 5 4 3				**67**

Fleck played steady par golf until the 14th hole, where he misjudged a 6-iron to the green and bunkered his approach, resulting in a bogey.

"I had a growing gallery up until that point, and after the bogey no one seemed to move," Fleck said. "I thought to myself, 'They think I'm done.'"

Fleck was now two behind with four holes to play, and few, if any, believed he could close the gap on the difficult finishing holes of Olympic's Lakeside course. But Fleck sent a spark through the crowd when he birdied 15. Pars on both 16 and 17 then set up the 337-yard par-4 18th hole to determine if he could force a playoff.

Fleck took his time walking to the tee, taking in the entire scene. Thousands of fans lined the hole.

"It was late in the day," he said. "The sun was breaking through the clouds. It was so serene. It was just like heaven."

Fleck chose a 3-wood for his drive on 18 but pulled his shot into the left rough. Luckily for Fleck the ball was sitting up, so he could get a club on it nicely. He pulled out his 7-iron because he wanted to hit it very high

with little spin so it wouldn't roll off the green.

"I hit it right on the sweet spot," he said. "The ball dropped out of the sky like a stone and stayed where it hit, about 7 feet right of the flag."

Fleck continued his trance-like play, taking less than 30 seconds to study the putt. He read the break and negotiated the speed perfectly, dropping the putt for birdie and securing a playoff against Hogan.

Hogan had politely acknowledged those who were congratulating him throughout the afternoon and also answered a few media questions. But he was clearly uneasy about the assurance of the victory others were conceding. Presumably to get a jump on East Coast deadlines, the media asked Hogan to come into the press room to recount his effort. But Hogan refused, noting the tournament wasn't over.

So convinced of the outcome, the NBC television broadcast went off the air well before Fleck finished, and the network turned down its option to broadcast a playoff.

"It was the loudest roar I ever heard," Fleck said of his putt at 18.

"They say it made the whole club-house shake."

That roar told Hogan all he needed to know.

Both men matched pars through the first four holes of the playoff, with Fleck taking a one-shot advantage on the 5th thanks to a bogey by Hogan.

Fleck increased his lead to three after consecutive birdies on the 8th, 9th and 10th holes. But by the time they reached the 18th, Fleck's lead was back down to one. All Hogan needed was a birdie to pull into a tie.

"Hogan pulled out a driver and I thought to myself, 'No, Ben, no,'" Fleck said. "I knew that you had to play a 3-wood on that hole. The driver would only get you in trouble."

Sure enough Hogan hooked his drive into the knee-high left rough. Error was compounded by misjudgment, and he eventually posted a 6 on a hole where he needed a 3.

Fleck played a textbook par (fairway, green, two putts) to secure his victory and one of the greatest upsets the game has ever known.

"I was thrilled," Fleck said. "Ben Hogan was my idol, and I was able to come in and do what I did that week."

BILLY CASPER

CATCHING THE KING

⚑

1966 U.S. OPEN

FINAL ROUND

*In a field of up-and-comers and wily veterans, Arnold Palmer looked to have the tournament in hand.
Yet golf's reigning superstar got distracted by a push from an aging legend who had briefly turned back the
clock. That left the door open for Billy Casper, who was able to quietly sneak up from behind on the back nine.
In a comeback for the ages, Casper upset "the King" to win his first U.S. Open title.*

B illy Casper didn't expect to win the 1966 U.S. Open. How could he? He was playing with Arnold Palmer, seven-time major champion and the game's reigning superstar. And through three and a half rounds, Palmer had put a stranglehold on the lead.

"I was seven shots behind," Casper said of the midway point of the fourth round. "And the way he was playing, there was no doubt in my mind he was going to win."

Complicating matters further was that Palmer had lost a pair of U.S. Open titles — both in playoffs — in the preceding four years. So this march to victory mattered a lot. Casper had all but conceded defeat.

"As we walked off the 9th green, I said to him, 'Arnold, I want to finish second,'" Casper recalled. "He told me, 'I'll do anything I can to help you.'"

With the lead well in hand, however, Palmer was thinking about someone else as they marched to the 10th tee: Ben Hogan. Palmer wasn't concerned about the 53-year-old who was playing one of his last U.S. Opens. No, the Hogan whom Palmer had in mind was the man who had set the tournament record of 276, way back in 1948. Palmer needed to shoot just 1 over par on the final nine holes to eclipse the long-standing mark.

Meanwhile it didn't take long for Casper to renege on his wish to finish second. He picked up a shot on the 10th hole, then

Billy Casper celebrates sinking a 25-foot birdie on the 11th hole during his playoff against Arnold Palmer for the 1966 U.S. Open Championship.

another when he parred the 13th and Palmer made a bogey, and he picked up two more with a birdie on 15 to Palmer's bogey.

The lead was now down to three strokes, but there were only three holes left to play. Palmer still had a formidable advantage, but Casper saw a glimmer of hope.

"He hadn't thought about me too much up until then, but now he thought about me," Casper said. "It was also the first moment where I was thinking, 'Maybe I could win this.'"

On the 16th hole Casper again made birdie to Palmer's bogey. Then, after another Palmer bogey on the 17th, the seemingly impossible had happened: the King's insurmountable lead was gone. If not for a great par save from the rough on the 72nd hole, Palmer would've lost in regulation. He finished 4 over to Casper's 3 under on the back nine. The two would settle the matter the next day (and Hogan's tournament record would live on).

Under sunny skies the golf world seemed back on its axis as Palmer led

by two strokes through the front 9 of the playoff. But once again the King seemed to lose his footing against Casper's steadiness.

After Casper birdied the 12th hole and Palmer made bogey, they were tied, and it was all downhill from there for Palmer. He made bogeys on both the 14th and 15th holes, then double-bogeyed the 16th, finishing 5 over par on the back nine. Casper went on to win by four strokes. It was Palmer's third loss in a playoff at the U.S. Open in five years.

"He didn't speak to me about that day for many, many years," Casper said. "I think that loss really hurt him. Regardless, he was so gracious to me that day, saying, 'Congratulations, Billy.' But you knew it just tore him up inside. As we walked off the green I put my hand on his shoulder and said, 'Arnold, I'm sorry.' I still think about it. He should have won that U.S. Open."

One of the greatest putters the game has ever known, Casper had one-putted 33 greens to win his second U.S. Open.

"When a golfer plays five rounds at the U.S. Open at the Olympic Club and he shoots four rounds in the 60s," Casper said, "it's pretty hard to beat that."

1966 U.S. OPEN										ROUND 1	ROUND 2	ROUND 3	ROUND 4	TOTAL
FINAL ROUND										69	68	73	68	**278**
HOLE	1	2	3	4	5	6	7	8	9	10	11	12	13	14	15	16	17	18	TOTAL
PAR	5	4	3	4	4	4	4	3	4	4	4	4	3	4	3	5	4	4	**70**
CASPER	5	4	4	3	5	4	4	3	4	4	4	3	3	4	2	4	4	4	**68**

Jerry Pate waves to the crowd after sinking a birdie putt on the 18th hole to win the 1976 U.S. Open.

JERRY PATE

WHAT COULD HAVE BEEN

⚑

1976 U.S. OPEN

FINAL ROUND

Jerry Pate's career will always be branded with a "what if." He showed extraordinary promise even before going pro, winning several high-profile events as an amateur. After finishing runner-up in the NCAA championships, he turned pro in 1975. If not for a horrible shoulder injury early in his career, he would've finished with more than just his 15 professional wins. All were won between 1976 and 1982 when his immense talent was on full display. His crowning achievement was as a rookie at the 1976 U.S. Open, Pate's only victory at a major.

I n 1976 the PGA Tour was truly in its heyday. Jack Nicklaus, Johnny Miller, Lee Trevino, Ben Crenshaw, Hale Irwin and Raymond Floyd were all in their prime and winning tournaments.

At 22 years of age, Jerry Pate was just a rookie when these giants roamed the Tour. He had received medalist honors (first place) at the 1975 PGA Tour Qualifying School,

the event players competed in to earn their place on the PGA Tour the following year. When he finally reached the Tour, though, Pate had no doubt he belonged with the big boys.

"It's all between the ears," he said. "Golf's about 99 percent mental and 1 percent talent once you get to the Tour. Everybody's got the talent to be out here . . . I had a lot of confidence in my ball-striking."

It wouldn't take long for Pate to prove himself.

In June 1976 the U.S. Open was held at the Highlands Course of the Atlanta Athletic Club in Georgia. The U.S. Open is notorious for being the hardest major championship to break par in, and as usual it looked as though even par would be a good score.

"A major championship like the U.S. Open or the PGA, I just loved to play

1976 U.S. OPEN FINAL ROUND										ROUND 1	ROUND 2		ROUND 3		ROUND 4		TOTAL	
										71	69		69		68		**277**	
HOLE	1	2	3	4	5	6	7	8	9	10	11	12	13	14	15	16	17	18	TOTAL
PAR	4	4	4	3	5	4	3	4	4	4	4	5	4	4	3	4	3	4	**70**
PATE	4	4	3	3	5	4	3	4	4	4	4	5	4	5	2	4	3	3	**68**

in them because I knew I could hit it in the fairway and put it on the green," Pate said. "And if you can make par in an Open and hang in there, you are going to be there on Sunday afternoon."

Come Sunday, Pate had indeed put himself right there. After the first three rounds he was just two shots back of John Mahaffey, who was leading at –3. Some stout names weren't far behind, including Al Geiberger and Tom Weiskopf.

In the final round, birdies would be few and far between. But Pate was able to collect one at the 3rd hole, taking him to 2 under par and one shot behind Mahaffey. That's where they both stood as they made the turn after nine holes.

After parring the first four holes of the back nine, Pate made a bogey at the 14th. That dropped him back a stroke as they headed to the 230-yard par-3 15th. With only four holes left to play, Pate needed something to happen. It did.

"People forget about how on the 15th hole I hit a 1-iron from 230 yards to 6 feet from the hole. I made a 2 there."

Mahaffey bogeyed the next two

holes while Pate calmly made par. Pate now had a one-shot lead as they headed to the 460-yard par-4 final hole.

Both players hit it in the rough off the tee, and each had a difficult approach shot over water coming into the green. Mahaffey hit it into the water, but not Pate, who had 190 yards to the green. Most don't remember the details, but Pate recalls them with the same precision he showed that day.

"When I hit the 5-iron, people were saying I pulled the ball," Pate said. "Of course. I am 22 years old hitting a 5-iron to a pin on the left side of the green. You can't go to the right. There was a creek up the right side. People forget about all that. There was actually a bunker left and long, so if you wanted to miss it, you wanted to miss it left and long, not right. And so when I hit the shot, I just hit the shot. I just stood up there as a 22-year-old and took a 5-iron. My caddie said hit a 5 not a 4. I hit it right at the pin and it was stiff."

That shot left him with 3 feet to go — an easy birdie. Mahaffey finished with yet another bogey, giving Pate a two-shot victory and the 1976 U.S. Open

title. His confidence had paid dividends.

"People don't expect a 22-year-old who is an unknown to hit a shot on the last hole to win the U.S. Open," Pate said.

It would be his only major championship in a career cut short by a shoulder injury. During some time off in 1982, Pate was doing some work on a golf course in Florida and was practicing some low-flighted shots with a 1-iron into the wind. He stuck the club in the ground and felt a pop in his left shoulder.

"I knew immediately something was wrong," Pate said. "That was the end of my career."

Pate was only 28 years old. He ended up having six surgeries over 30 years to try to fix his left shoulder.

Although Pate's chance at greatness was cut short by injury, the game's greats had taken notice of his incredible talent. The legendary Trevino once told Pate's wife, "You know, that guy right there was one of the great players in the game. He would have been a great player."

It certainly makes you wonder what could have been.

LARRY NELSON

A VIETNAM VET'S BIG VICTORY

1983 U.S. OPEN

FINAL ROUND

In 1983 everyone expected Tom Watson to be the first to defend his U.S. Open title since Ben Hogan in 1951. Otherwise, only Seve Ballesteros was thought to have a chance at victory. Among all the other afterthoughts was a Vietnam vet by the name of Larry Nelson. By then, 15 years removed from his tour of duty, Nelson had won the PGA Championship in 1981, but a second major had thus far eluded him. That is, until he putted himself atop the leaderboard through four rounds at Oakmont. With the title on the line, Nelson could only watch as Watson stared down a game-tying chip-in.

At the 1983 U.S. Open, Larry Nelson hadn't even played a hole and his prospects were looking grim. Eastern Airlines had gotten him to Oakmont, but his clubs had decided to take a vacation someplace else. Having nothing to practice with, Nelson borrowed a putter the same as his and proceeded to get to work.

"I've never spent that much time putting," Nelson said. "I didn't even start playing golf until I got back from Vietnam . . . I think when you learn the game as an adult you are more of a mechanical putter, unlike the natural putting skills of golfers who learned to play as kids. Circumstance causes the right things to happen, and in this case I was forced to putt — and it probably won the tournament for me."

Thankfully Nelson's clubs made it just in time for his first round. Not that it helped much. He barely made the cut, and early into the third round Nelson was seven shots off the lead. Favorites Seve Ballesteros and defending champ Tom Watson were tied atop the leaderboard, exactly as expected.

But Nelson's spot-focus and preparation eventually started to pay off. "All I could see were bunkers and rough. It was causing me to get tensed up. So I copied Nicklaus and picked a point 6 to 8 inches in front of where I wanted the ball to go, then

I didn't have to look down the fairway any more."

The tactic calmed Nelson and he went 7 under for the rest of the round. His 65 brought him to within one shot of the lead.

Paired with Watson for the final round, he watched as the defending champ birdied four of the first six holes. Yet Nelson wouldn't allow himself to lose his focus.

"I didn't care what Watson was doing," Nelson said. "I knew I had to keep hitting fairways and putting the ball in the right spot on the greens. On the 7th hole I was looking at a 20-foot putt for birdie . . . but this was a winding putt with 3 to 4 feet of break, and my ball went over the exact spot I had looked at [before it dropped]. That gave me confidence as I knew my putting was on."

Through the front side Watson's lead was three strokes over Nelson. But costly bogeys by Watson on the 10th and 12th holes narrowed his lead to one. After Nelson made birdie on the 14th, they were tied. Then on the 15th, Mother Nature made her presence felt.

As Nelson stood over a makeable 10-foot putt for birdie, a bolt of lightning struck. Play was called, but back

Larry Nelson salutes the gallery during a tournament in the early 1980s.

then players could choose to finish. Nelson decided to play on. He missed that putt and settled for par. He'd have to wait until the following day to make up for that miss.

Play resumed the next morning on the par-3 16th. Nelson's tee shot left him a 60-footer for birdie. It was his first putt of the day, but practice had obviously paid off. He nailed it and took the lead for the first time. By the 18th his advantage was two strokes. But this was the U.S. Open, and a title wouldn't come so easily. Nelson carded a bogey, leaving the door open for Watson — a birdie would force a playoff.

As Nelson waited behind the green with his wife, Watson steadied himself to chip from behind the green to tie. Not an easy shot by any means, but this was Tom Watson, the same man who chipped in for birdie on 17 at Pebble Beach to secure the 1982 U.S. Open.

At Oakmont, however, it wasn't meant to be. Watson's chip just missed. Nelson had won.

"I've got a great picture of me and my wife looking at each other," Nelson said. "It's a complete look of satisfaction on both our faces . . . I had won my national championship on the best course in the world."

1983 U.S. OPEN **FINAL ROUND**												ROUND 1	ROUND 2		ROUND 3		ROUND 4		TOTAL
												75	73		65		67		**280**
HOLE	1	2	3	4	5	6	7	8	9	10	11	12	13	14	15	16	17	18	TOTAL
PAR	4	4	4	5	4	3	4	3	5	4	4	5	3	4	4	3	4	4	**71**
NELSON	4	4	3	5	4	2	3	4	4	4	4	5	3	3	4	2	4	5	**67**

Zach Johnson lines up his putt for birdie on the 14th hole during the final round of the 2007 Masters.

ZACH JOHNSON

ONE FOR THE LITTLE GUYS

⚑

2007 MASTERS TOURNAMENT

FINAL ROUND

The pressure that comes with trying to win your first major championship can be crushing. Overcoming that pressure on a Sunday on the back nine can seem impossible. For those nine holes to be at the Masters at Augusta National, the task is unimaginable. But for a small kid from Cedar Rapids, Iowa, it was a dream that became a reality. On Sunday, April 8, 2007, Zach Johnson woke up with a chance to win the Masters. With Tiger Woods still at the height of his considerable powers, Johnson embraced the underdog role all week long and played a perfect par-5 strategy to walk away wearing the green jacket.

Zach Johnson receives the Masters green jacket from Phil Mickelson after winning the 2007 Masters.

For many golf fans, the Masters represents the unofficial start of the golf season. As the tournament approached in April 2007, the attention of the golf world was on one man: Tiger Woods, the sport's reigning superstar. Woods headed into the Masters having won the Buick Invitational in January and the WGC-CA Championship at the end of March (his warm-up before the Masters). It was almost a foregone conclusion he would be slipping on the green jacket for the fifth time.

Yet Zach Johnson had other ideas. Even though he had just one PGA Tour win to his credit (the 2004 Bell South Classic), he knew what his strengths and weaknesses were. At 5-foot-11 and 160 pounds, he wasn't about to try to swing with the heavy hitters.

"I am a guy that likes the underdog," Johnson said. "I am not a very big guy. I'm not a guy that is going to go out there and overpower a golf course."

Johnson accepted who he was as a golfer and made a decision that will never be forgotten. Measuring 7,445 yards in 2007, the course had two par 5s and two par 3s on each nine — perfect for players like Woods who possessed both power and finesse.

Distance wasn't Johnson's strength, but accuracy was (in 2007 he averaged 280.4 yards off the tee, which was 169th on the Tour, but hit 73 percent of his fairways, which was eighth). Knowing he could make up in precision what he lacked in power, Johnson decided he would lay up on all four par 5s at Augusta National — every single round. He was more than happy being the one in the shadows.

Augusta was playing firmer and faster than normal in unlikely conditions. It was cold, very cold for April in Georgia, and the wind had been howling much of the week. The average

FINAL ROUND

										ROUND 1	ROUND 2		ROUND 3		ROUND 4		TOTAL
										71	73		76		69		**289**
HOLE	1	2	3	4	5	6	7	8	9	10	11	12	13	14	15	16	17	18	TOTAL
PAR	4	5	4	3	4	3	4	5	4	4	4	3	5	4	5	3	4	4	**72**
JOHNSON	5	4	3	3	5	3	4	4	4	4	4	3	4	3	5	2	5	4	**69**

score in the third round ballooned to 77.35. Scores like that hadn't been seen at the Masters since the 1950s. Johnson's third-round 76, with temperatures hovering between 40°F and 50°F all day and winds gusting up to 33 mph, had put him in a great position at 4 over par. He was just two shots back of Stuart Appleby and one shot behind Woods and Justin Rose.

As the final round began, some early fireworks took place on what would be a historic Sunday. Bogeys by Johnson, Woods and Padraig Harrington and double-bogeys by Rose and Appleby swung the doors wide open for a bunched leaderboard. With Johnson's par-5 strategy in place, he birdied the 2nd hole. And on Augusta's next par 5, the 8th hole, Johnson again laid up, and again it led to birdie. When he made the turn with a −1 score through the first nine holes, he was +3 for the tournament and only one shot back of an already seasoned major champion in Retief Goosen.

"I didn't feel the pressure," Johnson said. "I didn't feel like I had to prove myself anymore, and frankly I still don't."

On the 14th hole, Johnson stuffed an iron shot just beyond the pin and calmly drained the 7-footer for his second birdie in a row. It put him two shots clear of the pack.

"I didn't really know what was going on," Johnson said. "I didn't know where I stood. I was still able to execute. I guess ignorance is bliss sometimes."

When Johnson arrived at the daunting par-3 16th hole — a hole he three-putted on all three days before Sunday — his caddie, Damon Green, finally clued Johnson in to where he stood on the leaderboard. A good tee shot and a birdie would put him three strokes up on Woods and Goosen.

With that knowledge in mind, his iron shot cleared the water and the bunkers, finishing some 10 feet from the hole. As if he'd done it a thousand times before under pressure, Johnson rolled his putt dead center. (It was one of only 27 putts throughout his entire final round.)

He stumbled a little with a nerve-induced bogey at the 17th hole, but he regained his composure with a world-class up and down for par at the 18th, and that was it. He left the course with a Sunday 69. Woods had two holes left to play, and he was the only one in striking distance. With a very un-Tiger-like par on 17, Woods needed an eagle on 18 to force a playoff. It wasn't even close. Woods holed out with a par on 18, and Zach Johnson was the Masters champion.

"It's mind-boggling to know I am part of that very small fraternity of guys," he said of joining the ranks of those who have prevailed at Augusta.

His par-5 strategy had paid off, in a big way. Johnson finished the tournament −11 on the par 5s, including birdieing three of the four on Sunday.

"It gave me the confidence," Johnson said of his strategy. "It gave me the realization that I can stay out here, that I can compete out here and I can get better."

Even after attaining his first major victory, not much changed for Johnson. After winning, he was asked, "Who are you?" to which he replied, "I'm Zach Johnson and I'm from Cedar Rapids, Iowa. That's about it. I'm a normal guy."

A normal guy with a hard-earned green jacket.

Trevor Immelman
lines up a par putt
on the 7th green during
the final round of the
2008 Masters.

TREVOR IMMELMAN

THE VOICE MAIL

2008 MASTERS TOURNAMENT

FINAL ROUND

There are three South Africans in the World Golf Hall of Fame: Gary Player, Bobby Locke and Ernie Els. All are household names in their home country, Player in particular. But for fellow South African Trevor Immelman, Player has been more than an idol and a mentor. He's also been a friend. Ahead of the 2008 Masters, Immelman received many words of encouragement from Player. And on the brink of victory, a voice mail from Player would help propel Immelman to his first win at a major.

Trevor Immelman celebrates on the 18th green after becoming the second South African to win the Masters.

Born in Cape Town, South Africa, Trevor Immelman began golfing at the age of 5. Shortly thereafter he met South African golf legend Gary Player when he came to Immelman's hometown and did an exhibition at his home golf course. It was a big deal.

"Gary Player, as you can imagine, in South Africa he's basically like our Muhammad Ali," Immelman said. "I mean, he is super famous in South Africa. Just to put it into context, he is as famous as Nelson Mandela."

Seven years later, Player came back to town to do a site visit on a course he was designing. Wanting to play a few of the holes, he invited Immelman to come and play with him, and a friendship began to bloom.

"At that point he really started getting involved in my career and really started giving me a lot of great advice from when I was a young man," Immelman said. "Not just golf advice, all sorts of life lessons that he'd learned over the years. I'm so very fortunate to have that relationship with him."

That was when Immelman was 12, and by then he was a scratch player.

Seven years later in 1999, Immelman showed real promise after winning the 1998 U.S. Amateur Public Links. Turning pro the next year, at 20, he climbed up through the professional ranks, all the way to the PGA Tour. He collected his first victory as a rookie in 2006, and by year's end he had won Rookie of the Year honors. Through his ascent his relationship with Player continued to grow, culminating in 2008 at Augusta, where the master passed on some important advice to the student.

Tiger Woods was the runaway favorite at the 2008 Masters. He had

2008 MASTERS TOURNAMENT FINAL ROUND										ROUND 1	ROUND 2		ROUND 3	ROUND 4	TOTAL
										68	68		69	75	**280**
HOLE	1	2	3	4	5	6	7	8	9	10	11	12	13	14	15	16	17	18	**TOTAL**
PAR	4	5	4	3	4	3	4	5	4	4	4	3	5	4	5	3	4	4	**72**
IMMELMAN	5	5	4	3	3	3	4	6	4	4	4	4	4	4	5	5	4	4	**75**

already collected three wins that season and had 13 majors to his name, including four green jackets. Immelman had only one career victory and was far from being in the conversation. He had yet to finish inside the top 15 in 2008 leading up to joining the field in Augusta. But the Masters was different.

"This tournament is such a big deal down in South Africa," Immelman said. "We grow up idolizing this event. Kids dream about winning this tournament, just as I did."

Immelman always played a practice round with Player the Tuesday before the Masters, and this year was no different.

"We had our customary practice round that Tuesday, and he was obviously trying to build me up, and pump me up, as much as he could about my game," Immelman said. "He was really impressed with the way my game was progressing."

That boost of confidence led to a great start.

Immelman's dream was beginning to look more like a reality after rounds of 68, 68 and 69. He was sitting at

−11 and had a two-shot advantage on American Brandt Snedeker and a six-shot lead on Woods, who was tied for fifth.

After his third round was finished on Saturday and Immelman had finished all his media obligations, he turned on his phone to find a voice mail from Player.

"[He was] letting me know that I was playing really well, just like I had been when I had played with him on Tuesday," Immelman said. "What was quite interesting to me is he said, 'You need to prepare for adversity tomorrow.' He said, 'Adversity will come at some point, and that is going to be the difference between you winning and losing.'"

Immelman didn't have to wait long for adversity to set in. He bogeyed the 1st hole and his playing partner, Snedeker, eagled the second. Just like that the two were tied at −10.

"I knew there was just such a long way to go," Immelman said. "It seemed like . . . there was disaster around every corner, so I was just trying to hang in there."

Immelman was patient. And things

did, in fact, turn around. Snedeker began to crumble, bogeying five of the next nine holes to drop to −5. By the time Immelman arrived at the 16th hole he had a five-shot lead. Not that he knew it at the time. It took a double-bogey at that par 3 for him to realize things were going well.

"I didn't look at a leaderboard all day," he said. "I kind of felt I was doing okay, because even though I made a double, people were clapping for me. I figured, man, this is not right, so I figured I was doing okay."

He was right. Despite his double-bogey he still held a three-shot lead. After parring the last two holes, Immelman became just the second South African to win the Masters. The first was none other than Player, who won it three times.

Immelman couldn't help but think of Player's advice the night before.

"It was very interesting advice . . . I didn't totally appreciate [it] at the time, but as I have gotten older, I appreciate it more and more," Immelman said. "I took that all to heart, and I'm obviously thankful for the message, and I'm sure he's proud of me."

MARTIN KAYMER

DOMINANCE AT PINEHURST

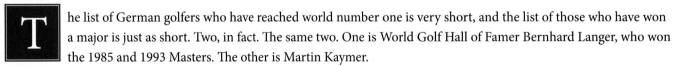

2014 U.S. OPEN

FINAL ROUND

Nearly four years after winning the PGA Championship in 2010, Martin Kaymer hadn't even sniffed another major, let alone a PGA Tour victory. Critics called him a one-win wonder, and many questioned whether he could find his way back to the top. But a Mother's Day tour win in 2014 — which he dedicated to his late mom — put him back on track. And at Pinehurst No. 2 shortly afterward, his game came together again on one of golf's biggest stages.

T he list of German golfers who have reached world number one is very short, and the list of those who have won a major is just as short. Two, in fact. The same two. One is World Golf Hall of Famer Bernhard Langer, who won the 1985 and 1993 Masters. The other is Martin Kaymer.

Kaymer won his first major in 2010, when he defeated Bubba Watson in a three-hole playoff to take the PGA Championship. But it would take him nearly four years before he'd win another. In fact, Kaymer didn't win another PGA Tour event until Mother's Day 2014, when he won the PLAYERS Championship. The win was extra special for Kaymer, who had lost his mother to cancer in 2008.

That victory came just a couple weeks before the U.S. Open, held at the iconic Pinehurst Resort. Nestled in the sandhills of North Carolina, the resort opened all the way back in 1895 and is home to nine championship golf courses, the most famous being Pinehurst No. 2. The course was designed in 1907 by renowned architect Donald Ross, but over the years it was changed, redone and modernized. Then in 2011 the resort decided it was time to bring the course back to its roots. After a year-long renovation by Bill Coore and Ben Crenshaw, the property had returned to the vision Ross originally intended.

So when Kaymer headed to Pinehurst in June for the 2014 U.S. Open, the discussion was just as much about Pinehurst No. 2 itself as it was about any player in the field. With the changes to the course, golfers would have to alter their style of play.

They would need to play the ball more along the ground and the contours feeding into the greens if they were to be successful.

Kaymer likened playing Pinehurst No. 2 to playing The Open. "Through any experience from the British Open, I've always done fairly well to putt [when the ball is] off the green. And I think a bad putt like this is still better than a bad chip, especially with the runoffs." Kaymer preferred hitting a bad putt to a chip because it would give him a better chance to get the ball to within 8 to 10 feet of the hole — allowing him a better chance to save par.

"[With this approach] you don't really make worse than bogey," he said, "and that's very important, I think, in majors."

The strategy paid off in a big way. After three rounds Kaymer was five shots in the lead at 8 under. He'd played nearly mistake-free golf and had put himself in position to collect his second major, which would cement his place in German golf history.

As the final round got under way, however, Kaymer felt he needed to keep his foot on the gas. Even though he had a big lead, he wanted to stretch it.

"You have to play brave," Kaymer said.

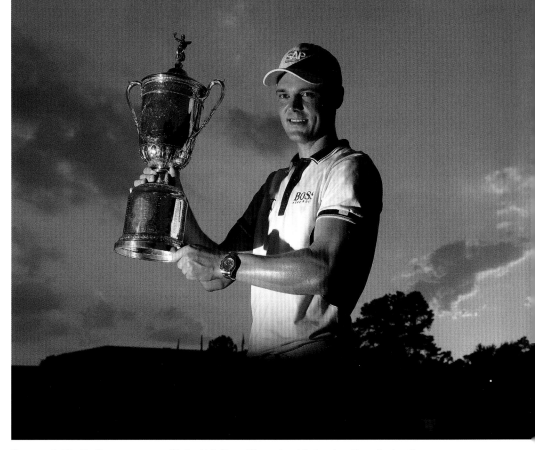

Germany's Martin Kaymer poses with the U.S. Open Championship trophy after winning the 2014 edition of the tournament. Kaymer is the first German to win the U.S. Open.

With that mind-set Kaymer shot 1 under par through the first nine holes and had increased his lead to six. Yet even with a six-shot cushion he didn't feel comfortable until the 13th hole.

"That birdie on 13, that relaxed me a lot," Kaymer said. "That was a big relief, because then I looked at the scoreboard . . . I thought, okay, seven ahead, six to go, that's fine."

Fine it would be. Kaymer played even par over the last five holes to finish 9 under for the tournament, an astounding eight shots ahead of second place. Kaymer had done it. He had won his second major championship.

"You want to win a major in your career," Kaymer said. "But if you can win one more, it means so much more . . . especially when I went through that low, [and they] called me the one-hit wonder and those things. So it's quite nice proof . . . It's quite satisfying to have two under your belt."

2014 U.S. OPEN **FINAL ROUND**										ROUND 1	ROUND 2		ROUND 3		ROUND 4		TOTAL	
										65	65		72		69		**271**	
HOLE	1	2	3	4	5	6	7	8	9	10	11	12	13	14	15	16	17	18	**TOTAL**
PAR	4	4	4	4	5	3	4	4	3	5	4	4	4	4	3	4	3	4	**70**
KAYMER	4	4	3	4	5	3	5	4	2	6	4	4	3	3	3	5	3	4	**69**

Wyndham Clark hits his tee shot on the seventh hole during the final round of the U.S. Open golf tournament.

WYNDHAM CLARK

PLAY BIG

2023 U.S. OPEN

FINAL ROUND

Wyndham Clark's journey to the 2023 U.S. Open championship was marked by profound personal loss and a fierce determination to honor his mother's legacy. As he faced the pressure of going head-to-head with giants like Rickie Fowler and Rory McIlroy in the final round, Clark's mental strength and confidence shone through. Despite some ups and downs, he clinched the victory, dedicating the win to his late mother, Lise Clark, whose belief in him had never wavered.

"P lay big," simple words of encouragement from a mother to her son that would resonate years later in a major way. The 2023 U.S. Open champion, Wyndham Clark, holds those words close to his heart.

"When she was sick and I was in college, she told me, 'Hey, play big, play for something bigger than yourself. You have a platform to either witness, or help, or be a role model for so many people.'"

Wyndham's mother, Lise Clark, died of breast cancer in 2013 when he was 19 and attending Oklahoma State. Although his path to becoming a major champion was marked with the emotional scars of a young man who had lost his guiding light, maturity brought with it a renewed ability to channel his mother's belief in him.

"[After her passing] when I was on the golf course, I couldn't have been angrier. I was breaking clubs when I didn't even hit that bad of a shot. I was walking off golf courses. I got out here on Tour pretty quick, but even those first few years I felt like I underperformed, and I've had many times where I've gone home and was yelling in my car and punching things and just so mad that I'm like, why can't I do what my peers are doing that I know I can play with and against and beat."

At times the pressure to live up to his massive talent was almost too much to withstand, and Clark contemplated his life's path, ultimately deciding that the golf course is where he is meant to be.

"I've probably had three to four really defining moments in my career since college, but I'm really glad that I stuck it through. And God has a plan for me, and it's obviously far greater than I ever could have imagined."

He owes much of that conviction to his mom's words and belief in him.

"I've taken that to heart. When I'm out there playing, I want to do that for her. I want to show everyone the person I am and how much joy I have out there playing and hope I can inspire people to want to be like me and be better than me."

In the final round of the U.S. Open at the LA Country Club, Clark showed that while he would start the day going head-to-head with two of the most popular players in the game, Rory McIlroy and Rickie Fowler, with whom he shared the lead going into Sunday and later in the round, his tenacity and a willingness to 'play big' at the biggest of moments would prove most vital.

"I guess it's nice being the underdog. It was great walking by hearing a lot of people chant for Rickie's name because it kind of fueled the fire underneath me that I could do it. My mental coach, Julie [Elion], told me, every time you hear someone chant 'Rickie,' think of your goals and get cocky and go show them who you are. I did that. It was like 100 plus times today I reminded myself of the goals. Now maybe they'll be chanting my name in the future."

Clark took sole possession of the lead right out of the gate with a birdie

										ROUND 1		ROUND 2		ROUND 3		ROUND 4		TOTAL

2023 U.S. OPEN
FINAL ROUND

										ROUND 1	ROUND 2	ROUND 3	ROUND 4	TOTAL
										64	67	69	70	**270**

HOLE	1	2	3	4	5	6	7	8	9	10	11	12	13	14	15	16	17	18	TOTAL
PAR	5	4	4	3	4	4	3	5	3	4	3	4	4	5	3	4	4	4	**70**
CLARK	4	5	4	2	4	3	3	6	3	4	3	4	4	4	4	5	4	4	**70**

to reach 11 under par, but it did not last long as a bogey on the next hole dropped him back into a tie with the ever-steady McIlroy. Another birdie for Clark at the par 3, fourth hole saw him regain his one-shot margin, which would briefly grow to two shots after a birdie at the seventh before another bogey at the eighth would see Clark go out nursing a one-shot lead over McIlroy. Solid par saves defined his inward nine before a glorious approach to the par 5, 14th found the green with his second shot that set up an easy birdie. McIlroy made bogey on the same hole in front of him, so a one-shot lead was suddenly three strokes with four to go, but the gravity of situation settled in, and Clark would bogey the next two holes, letting McIlroy back into the championship.

"That's the hardest thing. This is where the game is so mental because your mind starts to race. Obviously you turn and it's like, man, I should be at 12 or 13 and I should have a two-, three-shot lead. Then I almost eagled, made birdie at 14, it's like I've got a three-shot lead. All I've got to do is coast in and then you make a couple bogeys. So it's so mental because you

have to keep your mind so present. The minute you get ahead or behind, you feel like you make mistakes, especially at this level. It's more mentally tough than anything, but I feel like if you just stay within yourself, you can pull off the shots that you need to."

Professionals hate bogeys, no doubt, but sometimes at the U.S. Open, it's enough just hanging in until fate turns your way.

"I hit some great shots coming down at the end, and although I made a couple bogeys and it seemed like maybe the rails were coming off, I was pretty calm inside. I'm really pleased with myself with how I performed. Honestly, even after the bogey on 16, it's a tough tee ball. You hit it in the bunker. But I hit some great shots coming down on 17 and 18. I felt like I kept my emotions in check as much as I could until the green on 18."

Those emotions on the final green were cathartic in so many ways, but using the moment to honor his mother was paramount.

"Yeah, I know my mom is proud of me. She's always been proud of me, regardless of how I'm doing or what I'm doing. I just wish she could be here

and we could enjoy this. It was a pretty amazing week because my mom lived in LA for a few years, and I've had some people come up to me and show pictures of my mom when they knew her back in her 20s and early 30s when she was living here. I miss her, and it's obviously great to think about her, and being in LA and winning something like this makes me think of her even more than maybe my day-to-day when I'm not playing a championship. That happened that week, so it was kind of a special vibe all week being in LA. My parents got married at Riviera Country Club, so I have some roots a little bit in LA. But really, I was a mama's boy, so there would be a lot of hugging and crying together. But I know she'd be very proud of me. I really wish my mom could have been there and I could just hug her and we could celebrate together. But I know she's proud of me. You know, my mom was — she was so positive and such a motivator in what she did. She'd be crying tears of joy. She would just — she called me winner when I was little, so she would just say, 'I love you, Winner.' She had that mantra of play big."

Play big. That's what Clark did.

THE BIG PICTURE

Tony Jacklin hits a drive at the 1970 U.S. Open, which he won with a total score of 281.

TONY JACKLIN

THE CONCESSION

1969 RYDER CUP

SATURDAY SINGLES: JACKLIN VS. NICKLAUS

The 1969 Ryder Cup was held at the height of the socially turbulent 1960s, with the Vietnam War, apartheid and inequality among the concerns of the younger generation. The social unrest even spilled onto the golf course a month prior at the PGA Championship when a group of protesters tried to take their fury about apartheid out on South Africa's Gary Player. Meanwhile the golf world was experiencing its own bout of internal acrimony, and the two Ryder Cup captains did their best to incite dislike between the players. Thankfully sportsmanship won out in the end as the two sides played to a dramatic draw after an unforgettable battle between Tony Jacklin and Jack Nicklaus.

Tony Jacklin putting at the 1970 U.S. Open.

T he 1969 Ryder Cup was, well, complicated. In the late 1960s the tour players had broken away from the PGA of America to form the PGA Tour, while the PGA of America retained ownership to the PGA Championship and the American side of the Ryder Cup. One of the only prominent players who vocally supported the status quo was Sam Snead. Perhaps it was no coincidence, then, that he was named captain of the 1969 U.S. Ryder Cup team.

On the Great Britain and Ireland side was captain Eric Brown. Quickly labeled "the Fiery Scot," Brown wanted his GB&I side to believe they were every bit as good as their American counterparts. He insisted that they not allow themselves to feel inferior.

"One of the things he said soon after we arrived was, 'If their ball goes in the rough, you don't help them look for it,'" said Tony Jacklin. "I mean, come on. I was full time on the U.S. tour. Most of these guys were my friends. It wasn't going to happen with me."

The 1969 Ryder Cup was held at Royal Birkdale, a beautifully rugged and generally underrated links course in England. It had been over a decade since any team east of the Atlantic had won the event.

"The Great Britain and Ireland Team had suffered one defeat after another at the hands of Americans," Jacklin said. "[They] were seemingly bigger, stronger and better equipped to compete and dominate with their shiny new leather bags, well-heeled shoes and cashmere sweaters, compared to the relatively hand-me-down appearance of the GB&I squads heretofore."

The last time GB&I had won the Ryder Cup was in 1957. But 1969 was different. For the first time ever the teams would have 12 players a side and, as was the order of the day in late 1960s America, youth was served on the U.S. Team. The American contingent featured 10 rookies, including 1968 U.S. Open champion Lee Trevino, 1969 PGA Championship winner Raymond Floyd and multiple major champion Jack Nicklaus, generally regarded as the best player in the world. (Nicklaus would have participated well before 1969, but rules back in that day mandated a minimum of five years on the Tour before points could be accrued.)

On the other side, 25-year-old Jacklin was the GB&I team's biggest star. Earlier that summer he had won The Open, becoming the first Englishman to win it since 1951.

"I was brimming with confidence," Jacklin said. "I knew I could play with and against anyone. I didn't know I'd be drawn against Jack Nicklaus in the singles, but I was ready and so was he."

So was everyone watching. The 1969 Ryder Cup had been hard fought and often acrimonious. In total, 17 of the 32 matches concluded on the 18th hole, and five others made it to the 17th. The matches were conducted from Thursday through Saturday in those days, and on the eve of the final day's singles competition, the score was tied 8 to 8.

Singles used to be double sessions of eight, and Jacklin got the better of

Jack Nicklaus and Tony Jacklin shake hands after Nicklaus conceded the tying putt to Jacklin in an ultimate showing of respect and sportsmanship.

Nicklaus in the morning, defeating him 4 to 3. Overall, GB&I came away with 5 points to 3, giving them a solid lead heading into the final session after lunch.

In the afternoon Nicklaus struck first when he birdied the 4th hole, but Jacklin came back with birdies at the 6th and 8th. The lead would be handed back and forth two more times before the 16th hole.

Nicklaus went back up by one after Jacklin found a bunker with his drive at the 16th. Then at the par-5 17th, both players hit good drives. Jacklin hit a 2-iron and pushed it right, but it hit a knob and trundled onto the front of the green about 50 feet from the hole. Nicklaus hit a better shot and had about 20 to 25 feet left for eagle.

"I hit my putt and it went up and down the swales of the green and into the hole," Jacklin said. "It was remarkable. I mean, I was trying to make it, that was my intention, but there was luck involved, and seeing it go in was a great relief. It was probably the putt of

my life, one of those putts you dream of making."

Nicklaus then pushed his eagle effort off to the right, and once again the two were all square.

At the 18th hole, Jacklin and Nicklaus both hit 3-woods into the fairway. Jacklin went charging off the tee and heard Nicklaus call his name.

"'Tony,' he called, and he gestured me back with his hand," Jacklin said. "When I got to him, he put his arm around my shoulder and said, 'Are you nervous?' I said, 'Of course I'm nervous. I'm petrified!' Then Jack said, 'If it's any consolation, I am too.' That's the kind of guy Jack was."

Both players knew the fate of the Ryder Cup was squarely on their shoulders. Their match was all square and the teams were tied. All of their teammates were surrounding the 18th green awaiting the outcome.

Both players hit good second shots. Nicklaus was left with about a 20-footer for birdie, while Jacklin's 8-iron went to the back of the green

a bit farther away. Jacklin hit his putt to about 20 inches from the cup and marked. Nicklaus rushed his past the hole and left himself with about 5 feet for par.

"Being the great player that he is, he brushed it into the hole and as he pulled his ball from the cup, he picked up my marker," Jacklin said. "Jack handed it to me and said, 'I don't think you would have missed that, but given the circumstances, I didn't want to give you the opportunity to.' I was shocked."

Nicklaus later told Jacklin that he did it because, in the spirit of the game, he knew how important it was to Great Britain that Jacklin had won The Open that summer. He didn't want to dampen the revival in British golf and the hero they felt they had in Jacklin by making him the scapegoat for losing the Ryder Cup if he happened to miss that putt.

"I don't think I would have missed it and I was fully prepared to make the effort, but Jack always saw the big picture," Jacklin said. "That was the whole thing. That was his forte, all through his life, the ability to think clearly when the pressure was on."

The event ended in a draw for the first time in its history, so the U.S. retained the Ryder Cup. Nicklaus later became an important voice in the decision to add continental Europe to the GB&I team. Jacklin, who would later serve as captain of the European Ryder Cup team four times, is the man credited with rebuilding the foundation of the Ryder Cup into the massively popular and fiercely competitive event it is today.

Lee Trevino kisses his putter after sinking a birdie putt on the 15th hole en route to winning the 1984 PGA Championship.

LEE TREVINO
A FEARLESS MARCH TO VICTORY

1984 PGA CHAMPIONSHIP

FINAL ROUND

Lee Trevino's best days were behind him in 1984. He was in his mid-40s and already doing television golf commentary part time. His oft-injured back sure didn't help. Following his latest major surgery, he had stopped practicing altogether after doctors told him he had to limit the physical strain on his back. So Trevino practiced in his head, going over the mechanics of his swing. Heading into the PGA Championship that year, he had already won four career majors. So with nothing left to prove, and for one last shot at another major, Trevino let it all hang out, thanks in part to a little help from his wife.

Lee Trevino, earlier in his career, throws his hat in celebration after winning the 1971 U.S. Open.

B y 1984 Lee Trevino was done. He was 44 years old and hadn't won in three seasons. At the PLAYERS Championship that spring, he opened with a 76. After the round, Trevino complained to his wife, Claudia, that the game had passed him by. Annoyed, she intimated she would make up her own mind on the matter and trooped out to follow him the next day.

"I went out and shot a 66," Trevino said. "I thought she'd be impressed, but she looked at me and said, 'I don't ever want to hear that you can't play this game anymore. And I don't ever want to hear that you are too old to play this game anymore. You just shot 66 on the most difficult golf course I have ever seen in my life, and you are playing all these other pitch-and-putts shooting 78s and 79s. You are using it as an excuse.'"

Dutifully admonished, Trevino closed with a pair of solid 68 rounds to finish second at the tournament.

With his confidence renewed, Trevino rode that high into the 1984 PGA Championship a few months later. Overall, he was still feeling good about his game, but he wasn't quite happy with his performance on the greens. Then just three weeks before arriving at Shoal Creek Country Club, Trevino found a $50 putter in a golf shop in Holland while playing in the Dutch Open.

"I slammed it on the ground to get the lie I wanted," Trevino said. "I liked this putter. It was tough, like me."

In the first round of the PGA Championship, Trevino opened with a 69, one shot back of a trio of leaders. The second round saw Gary Player

1984 PGA CHAMPIONSHIP **FINAL ROUND**										ROUND 1	ROUND 2	ROUND 3	ROUND 4	TOTAL
										69	68	67	69	**273**
HOLE	1	2	3	4	5	6	7	8	9	10 11 12 13 14 15 16 17 18				TOTAL
PAR	4	4	5	4	3	5	4	3	4	4 5 4 3 4 4 3 5 4				72
TREVINO	3	4	4	4	4	5	4	3	4	4 5 4 3 3 4 3 5 3				69

thrust himself to the forefront with a 63. But Trevino posted a 68 to keep pace, and through the event's halfway point, the two shared the lead with Lanny Wadkins. Trevino broke the three-way tie with a third-round 67, with Wadkins one back and Player two shots adrift.

Sitting at –12, Trevino and his Dutch putter sent a message early in the final round.

"I sunk a monster 60-foot putt at the 1st hole for birdie," Trevino said. "I could have three-putted very easily, and I ended up making the putt. If I had three-putted, I probably wouldn't have won."

Trevino birdied the 3rd hole as well and was now two shots clear. It appeared that old Trevino was the Trevino of old.

But the other players weren't about to concede the win, especially the tenacious Wadkins. He matched Trevino's two birdies with a pair of his own at the 2nd and 6th holes.

After a lengthy weather delay, Wadkins made one more birdie at the 9th hole to reach 14 under, one shot clear of Trevino. After both players parred the 10th, Trevino made a great putt

for par at the 11th and then parred the 12th, while Wadkins bogeyed both holes. Now it was Trevino who was one shot clear of Wadkins.

A birdie at the 14th hole from 8 feet moved Trevino to two shots ahead, but Wadkins birdied the 15th to claw back to within one. On the next hole, the back-and-forth battle continued.

"I got in trouble at the par-3 16th, hitting my tee shot into a bunker," Trevino said. "But I made a great putt for par from about 20 feet and Lanny missed his birdie putt . . . Gary Player told me [my putt] was the greatest putt he'd ever seen under the circumstances. That was the turning point."

On the par-5 17th hole, Wadkins knew he had to get home in two. But he hooked his drive, and the ball landed among the trees. His second shot wouldn't deliver him from his peril, and he ended up in a greenside bunker with his third shot. Wadkins made bogey, giving Trevino a two-shot lead into the last.

Smelling blood and sensing victory, Trevino was aggressive at the 18th hole.

"I hit it into the short grass and went for the pin," Trevino said. "I decided

then and there I'm never going to play conservatively again. I hit it to about 15 feet and made the putt for birdie."

Trevino finished by kissing the blade of his putter.

"I wasn't supposed to beat those young kids," he said. "But I got them that day."

It was an impressive march to victory for one of the game's most fearless players. It's doubtful that anyone ever questioned whether Trevino was ever afraid when in the hunt. He seemed impenetrable when the pressure melted others. Even Jack Nicklaus, the most feared golfer in the game at that time, never got to Trevino the way he did other players. In fact, four of Trevino's five previous majors came in essentially head-to-head competitions against the Golden Bear.

Heck, not even Mother Nature could strike fear into Trevino when he was nearly fatally struck by lightning in the mid-1970s at the Western Open. Trevino came away scared of nothing and no one. Well, just about.

"I saw the light. I was done," Trevino said. "I know there's something more, so I don't fear anything . . . except my wife."

BEN CRENSHAW

FOR HARVEY

⚑

1995 MASTERS TOURNAMENT

FINAL ROUND

A player's first major is often his most memorable, and Ben Crenshaw's Masters triumph in 1984 is indeed something he'll always remember. But it's his 1995 victory at Augusta that is the round the 19-time PGA Tour winner will never forget. Shortly before the tournament Crenshaw lost his lifelong coach, a man he called "a second father." With a heavy heart, but supported by his good friend and caddie, Crenshaw played the round of his life to win his second Masters. His first green jacket was for himself. This one was for Harvey.

"**G**olf doesn't owe you anything" and "golf isn't fair" are but two oft-quoted phrases in the sport. They speak to the fickle, often cruel, realities of a game played with a club and a ball that has virtually millions of additional influencing factors, from players' own frailties to a conspiring universe.

At the 1995 Masters, fate had dealt Ben Crenshaw a harsh hand. His lifelong coach, mentor and friend, Harvey Penick, passed away the Sunday before the start of the tournament. Yet somehow, Crenshaw didn't just flourish through the pain. He prevailed.

"Harvey was like a second father, and a wonderful teacher and a great person," Crenshaw said. "To have played that well that week is beyond my comprehension. I didn't harbor any thoughts about winning the tournament that week until I got into the tournament and started playing well, and my confidence got up. But to have won my favorite tournament for his memory will always be my best moment."

Crenshaw flew to Texas for Penick's funeral and then back again for the start of the tournament. Under severe emotional pain of losing one friend, Crenshaw would lean heavily on another to get him through the 1995 Masters. At Augusta, Crenshaw had been using local caddie Carl Jackson since 1976, and the two had become close over the years.

"His possession of knowledge is unbelievable, unparalleled around here," Crenshaw said. "We have made a really good team, and I made a lifelong friend a long time ago."

He needed Jackson for more than just emotional support. Crenshaw came into the Masters having made just one cut in the past four tournaments that year, and he was mired in 69th on the tour in putting. Jackson took one look at Crenshaw and knew what needed to be done.

"He told me to move the ball back in my stance," Crenshaw said, "and to turn my shoulders more than I was."

After the first round David Frost, Phil Mickelson and Jose Maria Olazabal shared the lead at −6, one stroke in front of multiple players, including Jack Nicklaus. The second round saw Jay Haas assume the lead at −9 after a 64. Meanwhile Crenshaw took Jackson's advice to heart and augmented a Thursday 70 with a Friday 67 to sit two strokes back. Then in the third round a 69 gave him a share of the lead alongside Brian Henninger at 10 under par.

Perhaps Penick's gentle spirit was providing more than mere guidance.

"It was kind of like I felt this hand on my shoulder," Crenshaw said, "guiding me along all week."

To start his fourth round Crenshaw

An emotional Ben Crenshaw waves after receiving his green jacket for winning the 1995 Masters.

made par at the 1st hole to maintain a one-shot lead. Then after his errant tee shot struck a tree on the 2nd, he somehow ended up in the fairway and managed to make birdie. Crenshaw parred the next two holes, but on the tough par-4 5th hole he had his first hiccup of the round with a bogey. But, with resiliency as a subplot for the week, Crenshaw righted his ship with a bounce-back birdie at the 6th hole. After pars on the 7th and 8th holes, he birdied the 9th to reach −12. Crenshaw then made par on the next three holes as he reached the par-5 13th.

"I felt I had to make a birdie or eagle

there just to keep pace," Crenshaw said. "There's so much movement on a putt on that green. You might see 20 feet of break on a good distance putt. I made a good putt there."

After pars on 14 and 15 Crenshaw struck with birdies on the next two holes. He bogeyed the 18th, but his 14 under par for the tournament was enough to secure a one-shot victory over Davis Love III, who made a push for the lead with a fourth-round best 66.

"I believe in fate," Crenshaw said of his Masters win. "I don't know how it happened. I don't."

1995 MASTERS TOURNAMENT
FINAL ROUND

										ROUND 1			ROUND 2			ROUND 3			ROUND 4	TOTAL
										70			67			69			68	**274**
HOLE	1	2	3	4	5	6	7	8	9	10	11	12	13	14	15	16	17	18		TOTAL
PAR	4	5	4	3	4	3	4	5	4	4	4	3	5	4	5	3	4	4		72
CRENSHAW	4	4	4	3	5	2	4	5	3	4	4	3	4	4	5	2	3	5		68

Greg Norman tips
his hat in 1996.

GREG NORMAN

A WINNER EVEN IN DEFEAT

1996 MASTERS TOURNAMENT

FINAL ROUND

Greg Norman was the ultimate golfer of his era. From the moment he burst on the scene in 1983 until the ascent of a young Tiger Woods in 1998, Norman ranked top-five every year, including seven years spent at number one. He had his fair share of victories, including two at The Open, but many more seemed to slip through his fingers — none more so than his monumental collapse at the 1996 Masters. Yet despite that crushing defeat, the proud Aussie carried himself with the same grace he always did throughout his Hall of Fame career. And in the eyes of fans he still came out of it a winner.

Adversity builds character. Isn't that what they say? Perhaps it simply reveals it.

"If what happened to me, by my own actions, can help another through perspective and accountability," said Greg Norman, "then in failure I succeeded."

Over the course of his illustrious career Norman won 91 international events, including 20 PGA Tour titles. Yet for all his magnificence, he won only two majors, both at The Open. Many more got away, including playoffs at all four majors, often in devastating fashion.

Of all the losses Norman suffered, none matches his meltdown at the 1996 Masters. That was when he led by two strokes after the first round (when he tied the Augusta course record with 63), by four after the second and by a seemingly insurmountable six after the third. The fourth round should've been nothing but a march to his coronation, with Norman waltzing home to finally get his green jacket after a career of near misses.

Except for one obstacle — a wily veteran named Nick Faldo. In 1996 the 38-year-old was near the end of a long string of excellence. He'd won 35 times internationally, three times at The Open and twice at the Masters, both in playoffs.

Nick Faldo, right, embraces Greg Norman after Norman's six-shot collapse. Faldo's rise and Norman's fall handed Faldo the 1996 Masters championship.

To finish the third round, Faldo birdied the 18th hole to get into the final pairing with Norman on Sunday. Any other golfer would have been awed by Norman's huge six-shot advantage. Anyone, that is, except Faldo. The whole world might have already conceded Norman the green jacket, though not Norman himself. He knew he still had a lot of work to do.

"Everyone just assumed I'd already had it won," Norman said. "But I didn't sleep a wink [the night before]."

Norman bogeyed the 1st hole to start the fourth round, but no one took notice. Heading into the sixth he still had a five-shot lead.

Faldo birdied that hole and Norman's margin was reduced to four strokes. It might not be an overwhelming victory, the patrons reasoned, but Norman was still playing well.

Norman had birdied the 8th hole three days in a row, but he merely parred it on Sunday, while Faldo made birdie. The lead was now trimmed to three, dangerously close with 10 holes still to play.

The next four holes were perhaps the most agonizing of Norman's brilliant career. Faldo, who had already shown he wasn't about to go away, hadn't made any mistakes through the first eight holes, and Norman had begun to show some gaps.

The 9th hole was crucial. Norman's drive was fine, but his approach shot arched up onto the green and spun off. The ball wound up back down in the valley in front of the green, leading to another bogey. Faldo, meanwhile, still playing mistake-free golf, knocked his ball on the green and two-putted for another par. Norman's once-imposing lead was now down to two.

Back in the clubhouse several players

crowded around the television, scarcely believing what they were witnessing. Norman had finished the front nine in 38 strokes and was obviously out of sync.

"I was searching and I started tinkering with my swing on the back nine," Norman said.

The downslide continued on the 10th hole. Faldo once again made par, two-putting from 20 feet, while Norman's troubles continued. He missed the green left, chipped to 10 feet, then two-putted for bogey. His lead was down to just one. Faldo had cut five strokes off Norman's advantage in just 10 holes.

Then on the 11th hole Norman's lead disappeared completely. He three-putted from 15 feet away for bogey while Faldo continued to play steadily, making yet another par. They walked off the hole tied.

"Everyone assumes it was all mental, but it was more physical," Norman said. "Minor flaws in my game showed through on Sunday, and the problems compounded."

The 12th hole was one more nightmarish blur. Norman's tee shot on the world-famous short par 3 hit the bank fronting the hole, then rolled backward into the pond. He forlornly strode to the drop zone and wedged

1996 MASTERS TOURNAMENT

FINAL ROUND

	ROUND 1	ROUND 2	ROUND 3	ROUND 4	TOTAL
	63	69	71	78	**281**

HOLE	1	2	3	4	5	6	7	8	9	10	11	12	13	14	15	16	17	18	TOTAL
PAR	4	5	4	3	4	3	4	5	4	4	4	3	5	4	5	3	4	4	**72**
NORMAN	5	4	4	4	4	3	4	5	5	5	5	5	4	4	4	5	4	4	**78**

up to the green, two-putting from 12 feet for double-bogey while Faldo made another par. As the two walked to the tee on 13, Faldo had accomplished the unthinkable — he now was ahead by two strokes.

"I was in the Twilight Zone," Norman said.

Norman should have completely collapsed by then, but to his credit he came back with a pair of birdies in the next three holes and was within an eyelash of making an eagle on 15 when his chip nearly found the bottom of the cup.

Norman had finally righted himself, but it was too late. The imperturbable Faldo didn't lose any ground as he, too, birdied both 13 and 15.

Still two shots behind, Norman needed a miracle on the par-3 16th. Instead disaster visited him again as his tee shot plummeted into the water.

"I just tried to hook a tee shot in there," Norman said, "and it hooked, all right."

It was the final dirge of his funeral march.

In the end, though, Norman won over golf fans around the world when he graciously congratulated Faldo.

The two men embraced on the 18th green after Faldo had completed a five-shot win. He realized all too well the enormous difficulties Norman had gone through.

"I just said, 'I don't know what to say,'" Faldo recalled. "'I just want to give you a hug.'"

Norman proceeded to the interview room, where he patiently dissected the loss. Perhaps he was still in shock, but when he entered the room he strode in with head held high and his sense of humor still strong.

"I played like [expletive]," he said, grinning broadly. "I don't know any other way to put it."

On that day Norman showed his inner resolve in sharing what he told the media.

"I am a winner," he said. "I just didn't win today."

Back home in Jupiter, Florida, Norman spent the evening on the beach. There he relived the events over and over until he finally returned to his bed in the wee hours of the morning.

"After the Masters, I laid on the beach and I cried, because I felt like I'd completely screwed up winning a tournament that I wanted so badly," he said. "I think that's the only time that I've brought the emotion of a golf tournament back home."

It was, perhaps, the most disappointing loss of Norman's stellar career, but an amazing thing happened. In the midst of his darkest hour he endeared himself and won over a golfing public that could certainly identify with his grief, his fragility and his humanity.

"I received in excess of 7,500 letters," he said. "They kept coming in."

One could assume that Norman would love to vanquish that round from his memory, but somehow in losing he'd actually won something more.

"Winning is not everything," he said. "It is how you play the game and how you accept your defeats. I think that is the most important thing. I don't dwell, I really don't go back, good or bad. I think the next step in life is the first step — keep advancing, moving forward."

Norman lost a Masters no one thought he could lose. But his dignity in defeat helped define him as a champion in the most important game — the game of life.

Rocco Mediate chips during the fourth round of the 2008 U.S. Open at Torrey Pines.

ROCCO MEDIATE

HOLDING NOTHING BACK

2008 U.S. OPEN

PLAYOFF

Few, if any, expected Rocco Mediate to contend at the 2008 U.S. Open. He had missed the cut nine times and finished better than 36th only once. More than that, his bad back and resulting poor form even had him trying television commentary to test life on the other side. Add the specter of Tiger Woods on top of all this, and Mediate was the definition of a long shot. Woods would ultimately win the tournament, despite suffering a double stress fracture in his left tibia. But Mediate never backed down, pushing Woods right to his limit in one of the most memorable head-to-head showdowns in golf history.

H ow often do you hear about an unforgettable round that a player didn't win? Rightfully, history will record Tiger Woods' efforts at the 2008 U.S. Open as legendary. But no one had a better seat, or came closer to his own slice of history, than Rocco Mediate.

"I threw everything I had, everything I had," Mediate said. "He had to burn the last to stay in it again, and he did it. He's remarkable. But I hung in. I came out there in the middle, was three back, three down after 10 holes, and I really didn't play that poorly."

There always seems to be an air of the mystical about the U.S. Open, and never more so than when it is held in California. In 2008 a 32-year-old Woods was gimping into the event with a continuing array of physical ailments and surgery. Meanwhile 45-year-old Mediate had his own book of surgical augmentation, hope and rehabilitation. His back alone was as fickle and unpredictable as the marine layer of fog that rolls off the sea and often covers the host site, Torrey Pines, in an ethereal blanket of clouds.

Through the first four rounds, Mediate and Woods steadily ascended the leaderboard. After 36 holes both were tied for second at −2, one shot back of veteran campaigner Stuart Appleby. Then Woods did Woods-like things in the third round, including a pair of eagles and also a chip-in birdie on the 17th, that left even him shaking his head. At −3 after 54 holes, Woods led Lee Westwood by one stroke and Mediate by two.

In the fourth round Mediate's unwavering play almost got him the win, but Woods made a miraculous 12-foot birdie putt at the last to force a playoff. His celebratory fist pumps have become one of the lasting images of the championship.

After the round, Mediate was refreshingly frank about what had just transpired. "The thing that's most amazing is the man I'm going to play tomorrow has won 13 of these," Mediate said. "It's amazing how much it takes. I gave all of what I had today and I can't complain. I knew he'd make that putt." That putt took the two players to an 18-hole playoff. It turned out to be the last that would ever be played at the U.S. Open, as the United States Golf Association did away with this format in 2018.

Woods took a one-stroke advantage after the par-4 1st hole when Mediate made bogey. It was a bit ironic given that Woods had been +5 on the hole until that point, with double-bogeys in the first, third and fourth rounds (he birdied it in the second). After Woods bogeyed and Mediate birdied the 3rd hole, Mediate held a one-shot lead. But after Mediate bogeyed the 5th hole, Woods birdied the next two to build up a two-shot advantage. Bogeys by Woods at the 8th and Mediate at the 9th and 10th holes put Woods'

2008 U.S. OPEN
18 HOLE AGGREGATE PLAYOFF

	ROUND 1	ROUND 2	ROUND 3	ROUND 4	TOTAL
	69	71	72	71	**283**

HOLE	1	2	3	4	5	6	7	8	9	10	11	12	13	14	15	16	17	18	TOTAL
PAR	4	4	3	4	4	4	4	3	5	4	3	4	5	4	4	3	4	5	**71**
MEDIATE	5	4	2	4	5	4	4	3	6	5	3	4	4	3	3	3	4	5	**71**

SUDDEN DEATH

HOLE	7	TO PAR
PAR	4	
WOODS	4	**E**
MEDIATE	5	**+1**

Rocco Mediate, gracious in defeat, jokes with Tiger Woods following Woods' U.S. Open victory on the sudden-death par-4 7th hole.

lead at three shots. It looked very much like it was the beginning of the end for Mediate.

But strange things happen at U.S. Opens. Woods proceeded to bogey both the 11th and 12th holes and, suddenly, Mediate trailed by only one shot. Both made birdies at the 13th hole, but Mediate was on a roll, posting birdies at 14 and 15 to go up by one. After each man parred the 17th, Mediate took a one-stroke advantage into the last hole.

Once more, the par-5 18th hole at the South Course provided the drama. Woods would need a birdie to tie.

With the U.S. Open his to lose, Mediate hooked his tee shot, forcing him to lay up. Even so, he still had a chance to win the major.

"I had a putt to win on 18, and I said to myself, 'You've waited your whole life for it. Don't lag it. Just give it speed,'" Mediate recalled. "I just yanked it a touch. A little nervy. Tiger made his, of course."

With Mediate's par and Woods' iconic birdie, the 18-hole playoff ended with both players shooting even-par 71. The playoff moved to the par-4 7th hole to start the sudden-death stage.

"I had trouble with that 7th-hole tee shot all week," Mediate said. "I hooked it again in that bunker, and I caught it in a horrible place. So obviously it wasn't a very good shot."

Ultimately Woods left his birdie putt only inches from dropping and then tapped it in for par. After the trouble off the tee, Mediate needed to convert an 18-foot par-saving effort to extend the sudden-death playoff, but his putt missed to the right of the hole.

"I never quit," Mediate said afterward. "I'd been beaten down a few times and came back, and I got what I wanted — I got a chance to beat the best player in the world, and I came up just a touch short. But I think I had him a little scared once or twice, which was great. He said, 'Great fight' to me, and that makes it a little better, I think."

Phil Mickelson walks onto the 18th green during the final round of the 2010 Masters. His wife and family appeared at the 18th for an emotional finish for Mickelson.

PHIL MICKELSON

THE POWER OF FAMILY

2010 MASTERS

FINAL ROUND

Phil Mickelson had won the Masters before — twice actually, in 2004 and 2006. But his victory at Augusta in 2010 is deeply meaningful to the golfer known simply as "Lefty." Mickelson and his family had a turbulent 2009, with Phil's wife, Amy, and his mother, Mary, being diagnosed with breast cancer. He took time away from the game to be with family, twice. And although he wasn't as sharp as normal when he arrived at Augusta, Mickelson reasoned that all he could control was the moment before him. In typical Lefty fashion, his making an improbable shot helped him walk away as the champion and into the embrace of a lifetime.

Phil Mickelson raises his arms in triumph after his birdie on the 18th green at the 2010 Masters.

P hil Mickelson had a tear rolling down his cheek as he made his way to the scoring trailer at the 2010 Masters. "I don't normally shed tears over wins, and when Amy and I hugged off 18, that was a very emotional moment for us and something that I'll look back on and just cherish. I'll always cherish every moment of a very special week," reasoned Mickelson.

"Very special" was not the way the currents of the previous year had gone for Mickelson's family. In 2009 Amy had been diagnosed with breast cancer. After announcing it publicly, Mickelson informed the golf world he would be stepping away indefinitely to support Amy and their

kids, immediately missing the Byron Nelson Championship and his defense at Colonial.

While golf is seen as an individual game, the reality is that the players are one big family, and when one of their own is down and out, they come together. At the BMW PGA Championship on the European Tour, John Daly wore pink pants in support of Amy, while back on the PGA Tour the following week at Colonial, a "Pink Out" was held in which PGA Tour players and legions of others wore pink in support of the Mickelsons.

Thankfully, a few weeks into Amy's treatment, it was confirmed her prospects were good. Mickelson announced he would be able to begin

playing again at Memphis and would compete in the U.S. Open. But the Mickelsons' travails were not over. In July, they announced his mother, Mary, had also been diagnosed with breast cancer, forcing him to step back from the game once again, this time missing The Open at Turnberry.

All these emotions churned at the first major of 2010. Understandably, Mickelson did not come into the tournament in his best form, but with the hardest days behind him, he chose to focus only on what lay ahead. "When I get to Augusta, I get very relaxed and feel very comfortable, and I'm in love with that place and it brings out the best in me."

Mickelson opened the Masters with

2010 MASTERS FINAL ROUND										ROUND 1	ROUND 2		ROUND 3		ROUND 4		TOTAL	
										67	71		67		67		**272**	
HOLE	1	2	3	4	5	6	7	8	9	10	11	12	13	14	15	16	17	18	**TOTAL**
PAR	4	5	4	3	4	3	4	5	4	4	4	3	5	4	5	3	4	4	**72**
MICKELSON	4	5	4	3	4	3	4	4	4	4	4	2	4	4	4	3	4	3	**67**

a 67 and stood one back of the lead. A second-round 71 saw him two back after 36 holes, and a third-round 67 brought him back within one shot of Lee Westwood's lead through 54 holes.

On Sunday Mickelson was even par through the first seven holes. Westwood matched two birdies with two bogeys to stand where he'd started the day. "Westwood and I were walking up 8 . . . and looked up at the leaderboard, and we both said, 'Let's join this party. Everybody is having fun, making birdies, making eagles, let's get in it. Let's do it too.'" Mickelson would birdie the par-5 8th and draw even with Westwood atop the leaderboard.

Mickelson fought hard to make pars on holes 9, 10 and 11. "I'd made some bad swings on 9, 10 and 11, and I was able to salvage par. I was able [to advance the ball] far enough down by the green where my short game could take over . . . That's why I feel so comfortable [at Augusta] and I'm relaxed when I drive down Magnolia Lane because I know I don't have to play perfect golf."

It's known around the golf world that the Masters really starts on the back nine on Sunday. Mickelson

believes this too. And despite his rough start after the turn, he had a hunch that he had the game to win it. "When I hit that shot on 12 to a very similar spot to where I was in 2004, I knew that putt."

Mickelson's approach on 12 landed 20 feet from the pin, slightly above the hole. Not a good omen for many, but focusing on what lay ahead, he recalled his 2004 win and, just as he did then, calmly drained the 20-footer.

"That putt was what I had been waiting for . . . that got the round going."

At the par-5 13th hole, Mickelson hit a shot that would define the tournament and quite possibly his career. Having hooked his drive among the pine trees, he'd need the escape shot of his life.

Mickelson and his long-time caddie, Jim "Bones" Mackay, walked up to the ball and surveyed what they had left: 207 yards to the hole, a ball on pine needles and the only chance for the green through a gap to the left of the ball. To hit it, Mickelson would need to make the stroke blind, blocked by the tree in front of him. Add to that a green front protected by water. The

understated Mickelson summed it up thusly: "I was going to have to hit a decent shot."

Decent would be a layup to the fairway. What Mickelson accomplished was nothing short of astonishing. Setting up with his 6-iron, he barely hesitated and then gave it a ride.

"I just felt like it was clean enough that it was going to come out [of the needles] fine, and I wanted to hit something hard, so I hit 6. It came off perfect."

Mickelson's ball flew over the hazard and landed on the green, rolling to some 3 feet from the hole. Although he didn't make the eagle putt, the tap-in birdie put him two shots clear of Westwood, a margin that would grow to three by the time he made a final birdie at the 18th hole.

Amy had spent most of the week at home in bed in their rental house. Looking up, Mickelson saw his wife just above the green. "I wasn't sure if she was going to be there . . . her meds made it very difficult, and she didn't feel well or have a lot of energy. But to have her there to share the moment with my kids is something we'll never forget."

Rory McIlroy of Northern Ireland celebrates on the 18th green after winning the 2014 Open.

RORY MCILROY

RORY ROARS BACK

⚑

2014 OPEN

FINAL ROUND

*Rory McIlroy's major breakthroughs were his victories at the 2011 U.S. Open
and 2012 PGA Championship. Both were dominating performances,
so there was no reason to believe the good times wouldn't continue. Then life
happened in 2013. Amid personal and professional turmoil, McIlroy failed to
win a single event that year. He hit a low when he missed the cut for The Open
at Muirfield, and he continued his less-than-stellar play into the following season.
By the time the 2014 Open rolled around, it seemed everyone had written him
off as a potential contender. Everyone, that is, except McIlroy himself.*

Rory McIlroy throws a ball into the crowd as he celebrates winning the 2014 Open at the Royal Liverpool Golf Club.

H istory will record Rory McIlroy's 2014 season, in which he won two majors and a World Golf Championship event, as one of the all-time best. What makes it all the more remarkable is the adversity he endured just a year earlier.

In 2013 McIlroy got a new equipment sponsorship and had a very public and ugly breakup with his management company. After four wins on the PGA Tour the year before, he came up empty in 2013, even missing the cut at The Open. The start of 2014 brought with it mixed results and more personal strife. McIlroy called off his wedding with his fiancée, tennis star Caroline Wozniacki. And although he did win the BMW PGA Championship on the European Tour that same week, later in the year he finished well out of the running for the U.S. Open.

So coming into the 2014 Open, there wasn't much optimism for McIlroy's chances. Yet even through all the distractions off the course, McIlroy didn't question himself on it.

"I never had doubts," he said. "You can't doubt your own ability. All I had to do was look back at some of the great tournaments that I played in the past. The ability was still there. That wasn't it. It was just trying to find a way to make it come out again. But, yeah, definitely missing the cut at Muirfield last year was a very low

2014 OPEN
FINAL ROUND

										ROUND 1	ROUND 2	ROUND 3	ROUND 4	TOTAL
										66	66	68	71	**271**

HOLE	1	2	3	4	5	6	7	8	9	10	11	12	13	14	15	16	17	18	TOTAL
PAR	4	4	4	4	5	3	4	4	3	5	4	4	3	4	3	5	4	5	**72**
MCILROY	3	4	4	4	6	4	4	4	2	4	4	4	4	4	3	4	4	5	**71**

point. I never missed a cut at The Open before. And I really missed playing the weekend. I said to myself, 'I'll try to never let that happen again.'"

McIlroy's resolve revealed itself when he opened the tournament with two rounds of 66. At −12, he led the field by four strokes.

The third round was a peek at things to come for McIlroy. A couple of players mounted formidable challenges, and the Irishman deftly fended them off. On Saturday it was Rickie Fowler who challenged the leader.

Fowler's push to the front of the pack rested on the back of his strong start, where he amassed seven birdies in his first 12 holes. That put him into a tie for the lead with McIlroy. But on the 14th Fowler posted a bogey while McIlroy made birdie. At the 16th Fowler dropped another and was now tied for second with Sergio Garcia. McIlroy made eagle on 16 and led by an impressive five strokes. Fowler rebounded with a birdie at the 18th hole, but McIlroy made eagle again, and through 54 holes his lead was a commanding six strokes.

In the fourth round it was Garcia's turn to push McIlroy. The Spaniard made his move early with birdies at three of his first five holes. Meanwhile McIlroy fell back with bogeys at the 5th and 6th. McIlroy fought hard to overcome bad shots on the 7th to save par. Both he and Garcia parred the 7th and 8th holes, and McIlroy then made consecutive birdies on the 9th and 10th.

"That was crucial," McIlroy said. "That stretch of holes there — 7, 8, 9, 10 — was a big stretch of holes for me . . . Getting up and down on 7 was big. I played really good shots into the 8th hole and made a par. The birdies on 9 and 10 were big, especially with Sergio pushing there."

Garcia, playing one group ahead of McIlroy and Fowler in the final pairing, made eagle at the 10th hole to offset McIlroy's two birdies. Then on the 13th hole, McIlroy carded a critical bogey, dropping his lead over Garcia to just two shots. It felt like the momentum had swung in Garcia's favor.

But Garcia missed the green at 15. His approach shot landed in a pot bunker, and when he failed to escape on his first try, he was running out of time. He wound up with a bogey, while Fowler, who was still lurking dangerously, scored a birdie on 15 to keep himself in it. All three golfers made birdies at the 16th hole. McIlroy's lead heading to 17 was three strokes over both Garcia and Fowler.

At the 17th all three golfers scored par. McIlroy was able to coast home, knowing The Open was his to lose. Garcia and Fowler both posted birdies to finish. McIlroy calmly parred the 18th for the win. "Just a little tap-in, which was nice," he said of his final putt of the day.

In triumph, McIlroy had joined Jack Nicklaus and Tiger Woods as the only men since the start of the Masters in 1934 to win three of the four majors by the age of 25. Less than a month later he would win his second PGA Championship. Winning The Open had gotten him back on track.

"I was immensely proud of myself," McIlroy said. "To sit there at 25 years of age and win my third major championship and be three-quarters of the way to the career Grand Slam . . . I never dreamed of being at that point in my career so quickly. Especially being someone from around there, The Open Championship was the one you really wanted growing up."

PAUL CASEY

WELCOME HOME

2018 RYDER CUP

SUNDAY SINGLES: CASEY VS. KOEPKA

Success came early to Paul Casey both at home in England and abroad at Arizona State University, where he won three consecutive Pac-12 championships. After turning professional, his early success was validated by becoming the European Tour's Rookie of the Year. He amassed 13 wins on the Tour and three appearances on European Ryder Cup teams. Of all his achievements, being part of those teams left a long-lasting mark on Casey. So when a decade had passed and he hadn't been brought back, he was overjoyed to get another chance. And with a showdown looming with Brooks Koepka in Sunday singles, Casey wasn't about to let his team down.

Getting back to the Ryder Cup was anything but a linear path for Paul Casey. After being part of Europe's victorious 2004 and 2006 teams, as well as the side that faltered in 2008, he was passed over in 2010. Casey essentially took himself out of the running to be on the 2016 team when, a year earlier, he rescinded his European Tour card, noting his desire to reduce travel for the good of his family by focusing only on the PGA Tour. So he watched on TV as the European team lost the competition. Casey figured his Ryder Cup days were over — that is until captain Thomas Bjorn came calling in 2018 with the news that Casey was one of his captain's picks.

"Of all the golf I've played and victories I've had, it's amazing how the three Ryder Cups — sort of nine days of golf that I've been a part of — feature so heavily in the amazing memories that I've had," Casey said. "There's nothing quite like that."

Come the Sunday singles matches, the respective Ryder Cup captains determine when their players will play, but they don't know who they'll be playing against. In the Parisian countryside at Le Golf National in 2018, Bjorn benefitted from a 4-point lead on Sunday morning. So he decided to frontload his forces, sending Rory McIlroy out first against Justin Thomas.

Team Europe's Paul Casey eyes a crucial putt during the Sunday singles at the 2018 Ryder Cup.

"[Bjorn] was toying between Rory and me for number one," Casey said. "I told him, 'I'm not scared, I'll go wherever. I'm here to do a job.'"

After McIlroy lost to Thomas, 1 down, it was Casey's turn to perform. He had drawn Brooks Koepka, one of the hottest and most powerful players in the game. Koepka was coming off victories at both the 2018 U.S. Open and PGA Championship only months prior.

"Massive respect" was how Casey summarized his feelings for Koepka. "He's player of the year on the PGA Tour in my eyes, maybe even the best player in the world. You've got to give it to him."

Holding off Koepka was critical for ensuring a European victory. But things didn't start well for Casey. His approach shot at the 1st hole plugged in the face of a bunker, and his

impossible effort from there found the fronting water hazard. That put Koepka 1 up. But Casey struck back at the difficult par-3 2nd hole with a birdie putt from 35 feet to square the match. Such would be the punch, counterpunch nature of this heavyweight bout. Throughout, neither player held more than a 1-up advantage, which was Koepka's edge on the 17th tee. After Casey drained a 20-footer for birdie, they would tee off on 18 all square.

On 18 Casey hit a perfect drive and left himself with 176 yards to the final green. Koepka, perhaps burning from Casey's birdie at 17, outdrove him by an impressive 24 yards.

"That drive by Brooks just shows what he's made of," Casey said. "He's so cool and calm."

Casey left his approach 25 feet below the hole, while Koepka surprisingly pulled his 152-yard approach long

and left into a greenside bunker. From there Koepka got up and down for par.

Casey was faced with a 20-foot putt for birdie and a full point for his side. He narrowly missed, but he had earned an important half point for Europe, who eventually won the Cup, 17.5 to 10.5. In coming back late to split the match, he had validated his captain's faith in him.

"I was very proud to turn that match around," Casey said. "I threw a lot at him, he threw a lot at me. It was just a classic match."

In the immediate aftermath of his match, Casey tried to sort a myriad of teary-eyed emotions, clearly harking back to past hopes unfulfilled and his self-imposed exile.

"I can't stand watching," he said. "It's the worst thing in the world. To be back on the Ryder Cup team after a decade away, it's been magnificent."

ANDREW LANDRY

THE POWER OF BELIEF

2018 VALERO TEXAS OPEN

FINAL ROUND

In 2015 Andrew Landry no longer believed in himself and was ready to quit the game altogether. Yet even though he doubted his abilities, one person never wavered in her support. His girlfriend, Elizabeth, urged him to give the game one more try and go back to the basics that made him so successful in college. Soon after, and with almost no money left to his name, Landry picked up his first professional win, as well as an engagement ring. Three years later Landry finally got his coveted first PGA Tour win.

hey say that winning your first PGA Tour event is life changing. But what if it were your life itself that needed changing, and that winning on the world's most important golf tour was a by-product of renewed confidence and conviction?

"In 2015 I was going to give up the game," recollected Andrew Landry as he basked in the glow of winning the 2018 Valero Texas Open. "I said to myself, 'I can't do this anymore.' I didn't want to be away from my family, and I wasn't seeing results."

Having dark moments of doubt isn't shocking. Golf is hard enough when you're convinced you're capable. But sprinkle liberal amounts of skepticism into a steady diet of competition against other young, hungry golfers, as well as cagey, desperate veterans, and you've got a recipe for failure.

That was the place Landry found himself three years before his victory in Texas. He was done with the grind, done with the failed expectations, done with the lack of results. The comedown from his successful college career was debilitating. He talked to his girlfriend, Elizabeth, and told her he was finished with the game.

"She said, 'Let's just give it a year and see if you can go back to everything you did in college,'" Landry recalled. "I was a good player in college: a three-time All-American at Arkansas and a three-time All-SEC player with a lot of stuff going my way. However, right out of college it was hard — really hard — much harder than I expected."

Upon Elizabeth's suggestion Landry went back to using the PING equipment he used in college. He also returned to his old putting coach and ball-striking coach. It didn't take long for things to fall into place, in more ways than one.

Playing then on the Web.com Tour, Landry went to Colombia with only $1,000 left to his name. It was there, in a local shop, that he came across a pear-shaped diamond ring, exactly like the one he'd always dreamed of giving to Elizabeth. He gave the shop owner a $500 deposit and promised to come back, pick up the ring and pay the balance. Landry made good on his word that week, getting his first Web.com Tour victory.

In 2017 Landry got his second victory on the tour, and a year later it all came together on the PGA circuit. He narrowly missed his first win on the PGA Tour after a playoff loss to Jon Rahm in January 2018, but the final round of the Valero Texas Open in April was the culmination of a plan realized.

"Our strategy was to just go out and have some fun," Landry said. "That

Andrew Landry holds up the Valero Texas Open championship trophy following his two-stroke tournament victory for his first PGA Tour win.

was kind of our strategy all week — just have fun and be patient."

To say Landry was an underdog at the Texas Open would be an understatement. He entered the fourth round at TPC San Antonio tied with Zach Johnson, a two-time major champion, and one shot in front of Trey Mullinax, who had shot a course record 62 the day before.

But Landry started off strong, making three consecutive birdies to begin his round and adding another on the 6th hole. Another birdie on the 10th hole was negated by a bogey on the 11th, but the hiccup was his only

dropped shot over the final 36 holes, as he closed with all pars.

When it was all said and done Landry posted a score of –17, two strokes ahead of Mullinax and Sean O'Hair for the victory.

"I've learned more through times of massive struggle than times of success," Landry said. "We all do stupid stuff and make mistakes. But if you just work hard and believe in what you do and live a dream — just live a dream — crazy things can happen. I decided I was going to stay in the present, and that's kind of what I did that day."

2018 VALERO TEXAS OPEN **FINAL ROUND**										ROUND 1	ROUND 2	ROUND 3	ROUND 4	TOTAL
										69	67	67	68	**271**
HOLE	1	2	3	4	5	6	7	8	9	10 11 12 13 14 15 16 17 18				TOTAL
PAR	4	5	3	4	4	4	3	5	4	4 4 4 3 5 4 3 4 5				**72**
LANDRY	3	4	2	4	4	3	3	5	4	3 5 4 3 5 4 3 4 5				**68**

Jon Rahm celebrates on the 18th green after winning the Masters golf tournament at Augusta National Golf Club.

JON RAHM

THE FIGHTER

2023 MASTERS TOURNAMENT

FINAL ROUND

No one ever doubted Jon Rahm's fighting spirit, but his path to golf's summit wasn't always certain, despite his world number one status. Rahm is famous for his fiery competitiveness, but few know the unexpected source of inspiration that transformed his life. Through skill, determination and newfound English proficiency, Rahm emerged as a major champion. At the Masters, he faced challenges but remained steadfast, proving that on golf's biggest stage, doubt can be conquered with a fighting spirit.

Jon Rahm plays out of the bunker on the third hole during a practice for the Masters golf tournament at Augusta National Golf Club.

W hen thinking about Jon Rahm, many traits come to mind: fiery, outspoken, ruthless, tough, powerful, smart, sometimes impatient, and uber competitive. But the term that best describes Rahm is "fighter." However, "doubt" is not amongst the words that apply to the on-again-off-again world number one. But after Rahm secured his second major title at the 2023 Masters Tournament, he explained that his strut into golf's history books was not as inevitable as it seemed after his breakthrough at Torrey Pines two years earlier.

"The U.S. Open is about as hard a test as you're going to find," Rahm recalls. "And you know, I was never going to win a major unless it was at Torrey Pines […] All I asked for was a chance and I got it."

And the Spaniard might not be the global superstar we know today if not for the music of Kendrick Lamar.

Rahm's story, while not rags to riches like that of Lamar's, was, like the hip hop star, one of virtuosic skill and unrelenting drive. Rahm, a golfing prodigy from Barrica, Spain, was born in November of 1994. As a teenager, he won the European Boys' Team Championship in 2011 and then the European Amateur Team Championship in 2014. That same year, he was the individual leader of the Eisenhower Trophy Team Championship.

In 2012, Rahm committed to attend Arizona State University on a golf

2023 MASTERS TOURNAMENT
FINAL ROUND

										ROUND 1	ROUND 2	ROUND 3	ROUND 4	TOTAL
										65	69	73	69	**276**

HOLE	1	2	3	4	5	6	7	8	9	10	11	12	13	14	15	16	17	18	TOTAL
PAR	4	5	4	3	4	3	4	5	4	4	4	3	5	4	5	3	4	4	**72**
RAHM	4	5	3	3	4	3	4	4	5	4	4	3	4	3	5	3	4	4	**69**

scholarship. His head coach would be Tim Mickelson, Phil Mickelson's brother, who knew that Rahm had all the skills to be a major star. Rahm won 11 college tournaments — second in school history only to Phil — and was named the 2015 and 2016 Ben Hogan Award as the best college golfer in the country. He was the first to have ever won the award twice, eventually ascending to the number one ranked golfer in the World Amateur Golf Rankings. But still, coach Mickelson doubted his professional prospects due to his poor English skills.

"I don't think this kid is going to make it," Mickelson recalled telling his assistant coach at the time, thinking that Rahm might be a one-semester experiment. But Kendrick Lamar's album Good Kid, *m.A.A.d City* changed the course of Rahm's life.

"I became obsessed," he admitted. "At first, I had no clue what the words meant that I was singing. I just learned it. For whatever reason, the music just spoke to me."

And learned it, he did. His obsession with hip hop led to a breakthrough in his proficiency in English.

By the time of the 2023 Masters, Rahm was already a major champion, having won the 2021 U.S. Open at Torrey Pines on the wings of birdies on his final two holes. But the Masters is as much a matter of survival as a charge to the finish. While Rahm started the event with a four-putt on the first hole, he showed his tenacity by posting a score of 65, his best round of the week. The third round was delayed by inclement weather, meaning Rahm and the rest of the field faced the prospect of a long, grinding day. Rahm had to play 30 holes on Sunday, starting by looking up the leaderboard at Brooks Koepka who was four strokes ahead of him. Rahm appeared steely eyed for the formidable task.

"What is going on on the outside is not always a reflection of the inside," Rahm later admitted. "I was calm. I never got frustrated. I never really felt like anything was out of control. But obviously you're nervous, right. There's tension out there. That bogey on nine, timing-wise, was bad because Jordan and Phil came in making birdies, right. So what looked like a 2-, possibly more, shot lead, narrowed it down very, very quickly with the chance of them making a birdie on 18. So it made those 10, 11, 12 holes harder. Again, I might have looked calm, but I was definitely, definitely nervous out there. I'm glad that's the way it looked. That's what you strive for, right? You don't want to panic, and I never panicked. I felt comfortable with my game, and I had a plan to execute, and that's all I can do."

As to his fighting spirit, Rahm is comfortable with its role in his victory at Augusta.

"It's a little bit related to determination. I'm out there and I have a job to do. So I put in a lot of effort to try to beat the best guys in the world. So maybe that level of intensity and that determination is what you see, and that's why I'm characterized as a fighter. I'm also never going to give up. Even if I shoot myself out of contention, whatever, and I can finish strong to give myself a possibility to finish fourth; it's always going to be better than anything, right. So I wouldn't be able to live with myself if I didn't try my hardest on every shot, so maybe that's where it comes from."

It is amazing how a fighting spirit can overcome doubt.

PHOTO CREDITS

7 all photos courtesy of the author

USGA Museum: 76

Associated Press
Elise Amendola: 23, 158
AP Photo: 10, 12, 14, 16, 21, 46, 62, 74–75,
  78, 83, 90, 108, 110, 113, 115, 116, 121,
  144, 146, 149, 150, 152, 155, 172, 174,
  175, 176, 178
Mark Avery: 30
Mark Baker: 202, 204
Fred Beckham: 35
Joe Benton: 92
G. Paul Burnett: 84
Adam Butler: 8–9, 26, 58
Peter Byrne/PA Wire: 57
Michael Caulfield: 101
Chris Carlson: 32, 136, 186, 189
Bob Child: 118
Julio Cortez: 37, 128, 130, 131
David Davies/PA Wire: 56, 66, 68
Alan Diaz: 51
Matt Dunham: 60
Daniel Dunn/Icon Sportswire: 201

Ron Frehm: 86
Eric Gay: 138
Morry Gash: 156, 183
Scott Heppell: 196
Lenny Ignelzi: 188
Lou Krasky: 94
Pete Leabo: 19
Dave Martin: 184
Chris O'Meara: 49
Peter Morrison: 42–43, 64
Phil Noble: 126
PA Wire: 44
David J. Phillip: 4–5, 38, 72, 133, 138,
  170–171, 192
Ed Reinke: 28, 181
Charlie Riedel: 40, 54, 165
Eric Risberg: 24, 102, 104
Amy Sancetta: 29
Marcio J. Sanchez: 168
Phil Sandlin: 88
Matt Slocum: 2–3, 53, 106–107, 134
F. Carter Smith: 97
Paul Vathis: 81
Matt York: 70, 166

Reuters
Shaun Best: 160
Action Images: 99, 123
Phil Noble: 124
Carl Recine: 199
Joe Skipper: 142–143, 162, 190
Stefan Wermuth: 194

Cover
Main: AP Photo/Matt Slocum
Top Row (L-R): AP Photo, AP Photo/
  Phil Sandlin, AP Photo/Brian Lawless,
  AP Photo/Brian Rothmuller, AP Photo/
  Dave Martin

Back Cover
Top: AP Photo/David J. Phillip
Inset: courtesy of the author

INDEX